THE
LIFE

HARLEY-DAVIDSON

THE LIFE

HARLEY-DAVIDSON

DARWIN HOLMSTROM

FOREWORD BY NORMAN REEDUS AND DAVE NICHOLS

Brimming with creative inspiration, how-to projects, and useful information to enrich your everyday life, Quarto Knows is a favorite destination for those pursuing their interests and passions. Visit our site and dig deeper with our books into your area of interest: Quarto Creates, Quarto Cooks, Quarto Homes, Quarto Lives, Quarto Drives, Quarto Explores, Quarto Gifts, or Quarto Kids.

First published in 2017 by Motorbooks, an imprint of Quarto Publishing Group USA Inc., 401 Second Avenue North, Suite 310, Minneapolis, MN 55401 USA. Telephone: (612) 344-8100 Fax: (612) 344-8692

QuartoKnows.com

Motorbooks titles are also available at discounts in bulk quantity for industrial or sales-promotional use. For details contact the Special Sales Manager by email at specialsales@quarto.com or by mail at The Quarto Group., 401 Second Avenue North, Suite 310, Minneapolis, MN 55401 USA

10 9 8 7 6 5 4 3 2 1

ISBN: 978-0-7603-5564-0

Library of Congress Cataloging-in-Publication Data: on file with LOC.

Acquiring Editor: Zack Miller
Project Manager: Jordan Wiklund
Series Creative Director: Laura Drew
Cover and page design: Laura Drew
Page layout: Laura Drew and Beth Middleworth
Front cover photo: American musician (and actor) Elvis Presley (1935 - 1977) sits on his Harley-Davidson motorcycle on July 4, 1956, outside Memphis, Tennessee. *Alfred Wertheimer/Getty Images*

Back cover photo: Dave kick-starts his Harley-Davidson Panshovel in the twilight. *Ben Zales*

Printed in Canada

CONTENTS

FOREWORD By Norman Reedus and Dave Nichols

Norman Reedus is best known for playing the iconic survivalist Daryl Dixon on the AMC hit TV series *The Walking Dead*. Daryl is the sort of guy you could drop in the middle of the woods and he'd show up a month later, well fed and no worse for wear, zombies or no zombies. He's a survivor.

Norman is also a biker. Daryl often escapes from zombies on two wheels in the television series, echoing Norman's own love of motorcycles. This led to his TV series, *Ride with Norman Reedus* (also on AMC). Each episode revolves around Norman riding with friends and artists—for example, *Easy Rider* star Peter Fonda—to incredibly cool locations on amazing motorcycles.

"I've been into bikes since I was a teenager," Norman says. "Motorcycles offer me a way to get away from it all. To escape."

This book is an attempt to put some of those feelings of freedom and escape into words and pictures. More than a history of Harley-Davidson or of biker culture, it captures some of the essence of what riding is all about. "For me, motorcycles are linked to my own sense of personal freedom," Norman says. "You're just there with yourself and you think and come up with ideas. I do my best thinking on a motorcycle."

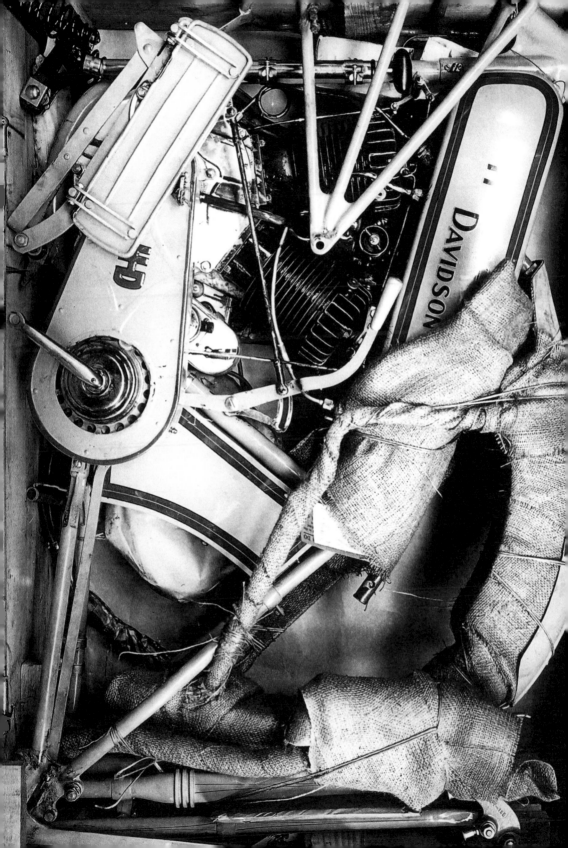

INTRODUCTION

The boy and his sister stepped out the door of the High Plains gas station on a hot August evening, savoring the popsicles their mother had bought them while they waited for the station owner to fix the flat tire on their Ford wagon. The kids relished the respite from the confines of the wagon's back seat, enduring the agony of puberty, close quarters, and their parents' endless-loop soundtrack of The Captain & Tennille, Tony Orlando, and Barbra Streisand wafting from the cassette deck.

City kids, they weren't impressed by lectures from park rangers explaining the importance of sphagnum peat moss in the great cycle of life, but the thing that they sensed coming down the road was far from boring. They felt it in the soles of their Keds before they heard its thunder, before they saw a point appear on the horizon, growing larger as the beat grew louder. The point became a pack of motorcycles, so loud the kids could feel each piston stroke of the big V-twin engines in their guts. The pack pulled into the gas station and riders began fueling their machines. The station owner's wife appeared from the office clutching a broom like a weapon. She looked frightened, but the children were transfixed by the spectacle.

The bikers smiled at the kids. They'd been there themselves, longing for the joy and the freedom that can only be found riding a powerful motorcycle down an open road. They recognized the look on the youngsters' faces. They knew that, from this point on, these kids would be hooked on the life Harley-Davidson.

THE LIFE-HISTORIC

EXPANDING THE GENE POOL

The life Harley-Davidson began at the turn of the twentieth century, an era in which people were transfixed by the prospect of internal combustion-powered mobility. Throughout human history, most people lived and died within walking distance of their birthplace. Even after the advent of mass transit, in the form of ships and later trains, individual mobility was unobtainable for most people. While cinematic Westerns create the illusion of a nation of cowboys rambling across the prairies on their horses, the reality was that the horse as a form of transportation was far from practical for the average person.

That changed in 1885 with the invention of the safety bicycle, featuring two same-sized tires that made it much safer and more stable than the earlier high-wheeled "penny-farthing" bicycles. A central crank that drove the rear wheel allowed variation in gear ratios, giving a rider the ability to cover greater distances. The safety bicycle was soon eclipsed in the public's imagination by the more romantic motorized bicycle, but the impact the safety bicycle had on the average person's life cannot be overstated. Prior to the safety bicycle, going into town from the countryside was an epic production, undertaken only to procure necessary supplies. Hitching a team of horses to a wagon was itself an involved procedure, taking up much of the morning. Then the ride into town could be a daylong ordeal (depending on the distance traveled), which meant that the farmer would have to get a hotel room in town after stocking up on flour, coffee, whiskey, and other essentials at the general store.

The safety bicycle gave a rider the ability to ride to town in less time that it took to round up the horses and hitch them to the wagon. Going to town went from being a two-day ordeal to something a person could do in an afternoon. Suddenly, Will Parker could, if he had a free afternoon, ride his bicycle to town and court Ado Annie Carnes, or some other gal "who cain't say no," thus expanding the gene pool and changing humanity at a cellular level.

SCARING THE HORSES

The work of Gottlieb Daimler and Wilhelm Maybach made short work of the safety bicycle's status as the premiere form of personal transportation. In 1885, the same year the safety bicycle was invented, Daimler and Maybach patented a four-stroke internal-combustion engine, which they tested on a vehicle they called the *Reitwagen* ("riding wagon"). The Reitwagen was also known as the *Einspur*, or "single-track," because, like the bicycle, it had just two wheels. This meant that the world's first internal combustion vehicle was a motorcycle.

Bicycle sales boomed in the last years of the nineteenth century. At the dawn of the twentieth century, though, motorcycles were starting to appear around the world. By 1901, this marvel of modernity had made its way to Milwaukee, where a motorcycle caught the attention of 20-year-old Bill Harley. By July of that year, Harley had drawn up plans for a bicycle motor. Working on the project with Arthur Davidson and another buddy named Henry Melk (who owned a lathe), Bill and Art tinkered on their contraption throughout 1902 and into 1903.

Anxious to ride their new machine, Art's brother Walter cleared a space in his father's backyard work shed and went to work helping Art and

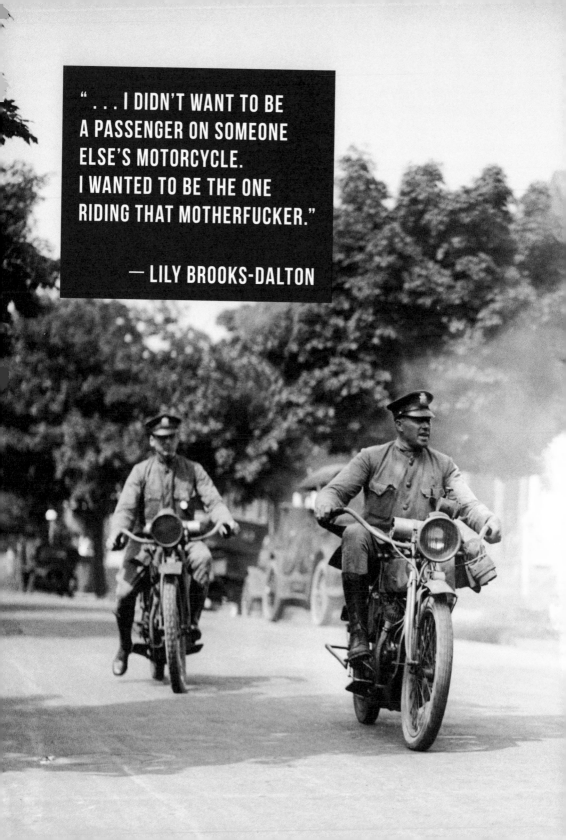

" . . . I DIDN'T WANT TO BE A PASSENGER ON SOMEONE ELSE'S MOTORCYCLE. I WANTED TO BE THE ONE RIDING THAT MOTHERFUCKER."

— LILY BROOKS-DALTON

Bill finish the project. Harley and the Davidson brothers began testing their creation that summer. While the motor-bicycle worked, its motor wasn't powerful enough, so the boys developed a second motorcycle, with a sturdy loop-frame replacing the original's flimsy bicycle frame. More importantly, a bigger motor that incorporated technical advances pioneered by Arthur's friend, outboard-motor builder Ole Evinrude, gave the motorcycle the power to climb the hilly streets of Milwaukee. The sight of Harley and the Davidson brothers roaring around Milwaukee aboard their motorcycle scared the bejesus out of the horses, but it inspired like-minded thrill seekers to get motorcycles of their own. Sometime in 1904, a friend of the boys named Henry Meyer bought their first machine, motivating the young men to build more motorcycles. The next year, Harley and the Davidsons built at least five motorcycles, three of which a Chicago motorcycle aficionado named Carl H. Lang sold in his hometown. This led to the production of even more motorcycles; late in 1906, Harley and the Davidsons built a small factory on Juneau Avenue (then Chestnut Street), marking the birth of the Harley-Davidson Motor Company as a full-fledged industrial concern.

TIN LIZZIE THREAT

Harley-Davidson had built the right product for the time, and sales skyrocketed. In 1907, Harley built 157 motorcycles; 1908 saw 456, then 1,149 in 1909, 3,168 in 1910, and 5,625 in 1911. It seemed like up was the only direction production could go. After a decline in 1912, production in 1913 shot up to 12,966 motorcycles. Output continued to grow until 1920, when it topped out at 28,189 motorcycles. In 1921, production fell to 10,202 motorcycles; it wouldn't rise above 28,000 units again until the 1970s. So what happened? Henry Ford's Model T happened. In the early years of internal-combustion vehi-

cle sales, motorcycles outsold automobiles because two-wheeled vehicles were much cheaper than four-wheeled vehicles. That changed forever on December 1, 1913, when Ford Motor Company cranked up the world's first moving assembly line for automobile production. This allowed for a dramatic increase in the production of the company's popular Model T car, accompanied by an equally dramatic decrease in retail pricing. In 1909, Ford sold 10,666 Model Ts at a price of $825 per unit. In 1913, production jumped to 170,211 units and the price fell to $525. By 1916, production increased to 501,462 units and the price of a Model T fell to $345. A basic Harley-Davidson twin, the Model 11-J, cost $310 in 1915, and a few basic accessories like headlights and a horn could push the price above that of a Model T. The automobile was not only infinitely more useful and practical: it now cost the same as a motorcycle. The automobile had replaced the motorcycle as the most basic form of transportation.

HARLEY AT WAR

> "BIKERS AND VETERANS GO HAND IN HAND AND I CAN ASSURE YOU THAT WE NEVER FORGET. THAT RUMBLING SOUND YOU HEAR WHEN A GROUP OF BIKES COME TOGETHER IS NOT NOISE SIR, IT IS THE HARMONY OF BROTHERHOOD COMING TOGETHER FOR A PURPOSE AND CAUSE."
>
> —CRYSTA BAKER

Despite the ascendance of the automobile, things were going well in Milwaukee as the 1930s gave way to the 1940s. The country was slowly emerging from the Great Depression, and Harley's ground-breaking Knucklehead superbike (introduced in 1936) was selling well. Harley sold 2,695 of its big overhead-valve twins in 1939 and, by 1941, that number had jumped to 5,149. That was the peak, though: in 1942, Harley sold just 1,742 Knuckleheads; in 1943, that number fell to zero, thanks to a psychotic Austrian, then chancellor of Germany, and his allies in Japan. After Japan bombed Pearl Harbor on December 7, 1941 and drew the United States into World War II, civilian vehicle production stopped. All US manufacturing capabilities were diverted to producing war material.

Initially, that material included motorcycles—lots of motorcycles. Since the turn of the twentieth century, motorcycles had proven extremely useful in combat. They were light, simple, agile, and quick. They served couriers bringing information to and from the battle lines, and they were handy for getting troops in and out of combat. And, of course, they weren't spooked by loud noises as were the horses they quickly replaced. Historically, war was a gold mine for motorcycle manufacturers and, as World War II ramped up, it seemed this new conflict would be no exception.

Harley began developing a more sophisticated model, a shaft-driven opposed twin based on the BMWs that had been performing well in the African theater, but production of that model ended before 1,000 were built. In fact, the age of motorcycles as tools of war ended rather abruptly thanks to the introduction of the Jeep. The Jeep was little more than a simple, rugged, four-wheel-drive motorized cart, but it was far more practical than any motorcycle. It could carry as many people as could climb on its flat surfaces, it could go just about anywhere because of its light weight and four-wheel-drive, and anyone who could drive a car could drive a Jeep. Compare this with a motorcycle, which required a specialized skill set to ride, and it's easy to see why the Jeep became the preferred military vehicle. Harley went on to build a handful of WLA models for the military during the Korean war, but by then the motorcycle was more of a military novelty than a useful tool. While Harley had a brief financial windfall from the initial sales of its military motorcycles, the long-term effects of the war proved mixed. Harley's factory kept busy during the war, but when post-war civilian motorcycle production resumed, materials were scarce. The United States devoted much of its resources toward rebuilding Europe as part of the Marshall Plan, diverting resources away from domestic manufacturers. Early postwar Harleys lacked the chrome trim and other amenities that the prewar versions had featured.

WAR BOOTY

Big twin-cylinder motorcycles have made up the bulk of Harley-Davidson's production since the company's earliest years. Harley's first V-twin, the 1909 Model 5-D, incorporated most of the characteristics that would define Harley-Davidson engines for the next 100-plus years, such as the forty-five-degree V angle and a single carburetor nestled between the cylinders, but it had one feature that wouldn't make the cut: atmospheric intake valves. This crude system was the industry standard, sufficient for the single-cylinder engines of the day but wholly inadequate for Harley's new large-displacement twin. Two years later, Harley rectified that problem and introduced the Model 8-X-E, which had proper mechanically operated valves. The model was a success and soon big twins comprised the bulk of Harley's sales.

The big twins outsold the singles, and they also generated better profit margins, motivating Harley to focus on developing the larger bikes. The company didn't completely ignore the smaller singles that were needed to attract new riders, but, after a series of slow-selling singles, Harley threw in the towel and ceased producing small-displacement motorcycles in the late 1930s.

After World War II, returning soldiers began procreating like rabbits, resulting in a huge potential customer base for Harley-Davidson. This posed a challenge for the company, since Harley had no small, inexpensive motorcycles available for this tsunami of new buyers. The solution came in the form of war booty brought back from Germany. As part of that country's war reparations, Harley seized the designs and tooling needed to build a 125-cubic-centimeter, two-stroke engine from German maker DKW. This was the ideal engine

> **"IT WASN'T UNTIL I WENT TO COLLEGE AND I GOT MY FIRST MOTORCYCLE THAT I UNDERSTOOD THE THRILL OF SPEED."**
>
> **—VIN DIESEL**

small motorcycles for the roughly 76 million youngsters who would soon come to be known as "baby boomers."

For the 1948 model year, Harley mounted its Germanic engine in a cute little motorcycle, the Model S. The 1.7-horsepower engine could get the miniature motorcycle moving at 35 to 40 miles per hour, at least in theory. In reality, a strong tailwind helped, as did a steep decline. It was fast enough to have fun, but not fast enough to get a rider in serious trouble. Harley sold 10,117 of the little buggers at $325 a pop. The Model S was followed by a 165-cubic-centimeter version, called the Model ST. The smaller Model was renamed the "Hummer" for the 1955 model year. In the swinging '60s, that name would take on a more provocative meaning, but in the more-innocent 1950s a Hummer was still just a fun little motorbike. An onslaught of light, powerful imported motorcycles, first from England and later from Japan, killed the market for Harley's ST and Hummer, and Harley phased out its two-stroke motorcycles after the 1966 model year.

ELVIS PRESLEY: THE ULTIMATE ENTHUSIAST

Even as a boy, Elvis Presley loved motorcycles, but his parents were so poor that they couldn't afford to buy him a bicycle, much less a motorcycle. On January 8, 1946, they did manage to scrape together $12.95 to buy Elvis his first guitar, a device Elvis's mother, Gladys, deemed safer than a bicycle or, God forbid, a motorcycle. Although the 11-year-old would have much preferred a motorcycle, that $12.95 turned out to be money well spent; in 1955, Elvis parlayed that investment into enough money to buy the motorcycle he really wanted: an S-series Harley with a 165cc two-stroke engine.

The music thing seemed to be working out for young Elvis. On November 20, 1955, he signed a contract with RCA Records, enabling him to upgrade to Harley's newest model in January 1956: a Pepper-Red-and-White Model KH from Memphis, Tennessee, dealer Tommy Taylor. Elvis paid $903.19, including the trade-in amount from his S-series Harley. Even though Elvis was earning enough to make ends meet from his music, he still had to make payments of $47 a month on his new bike. The full list price for the KH was $925 plus $75.75 for the Deluxe Group option package. The buddy seat cost an additional $18, plus $15.25 for the windshield. The grand total for the motorcycle was $1,034, meaning his trade-in was worth about $110. This marked the last time in his life that Elvis had to pinch pennies. Before the year ended, he had enough money to buy a top-of-the-line Harley-Davidson FL, a bike that would be followed by many, many more Harleys over the years. This time, he didn't have to trade in his old bike and make

> "THE MOST LOVED BIKE ELVIS OWNED WAS THE HARLEY DRESSER. BIGGER AND CLOSE TO THE GROUND: JUST WHAT ELVIS LOVED."
>
> —RON ELLIOT, SUPER CYCLE MOTORCYCLES

payments on an installment plan. Instead, he gave the KH to his riding buddy, Flemming Horn as a gift, but not before appearing aboard it on the cover of the May 1956 issue of *The Enthusiast*, Harley-Davidson's official magazine.

Elvis had wanted a motorcycle longer than he'd wanted to be a pop star, and he remained an avid motorcyclist until his untimely death, though in later years his deteriorating physical condition confined him to three wheels rather than two. As he became more isolated by his fame, his Harleys provided a much-needed escape. Elvis loved nothing more than to get away from the insanity of life as a superstar aboard his motorcycles, exchanging the fawning praise of sycophants and business partners for the life Harley-Davidson, hitting the open road where he could feel the wind in his famous pompadour. When his fame grew so great that he was unable to ride in broad daylight without causing traffic accidents, he would go riding at night, escaping under the cover of darkness.

HARLEY ALFREDO

In the years following World War II Harley met the demand for small, inexpensive motorcycles with German-sourced two-strokes, but by the mid-1950s, the 20-plus-year-old engine was long past its use-by date. The timing couldn't have been worse, because the massive procreation orgy in which returning war vets engaged meant that tens of millions of young people were now old enough to pester their parents about buying them motorcycles. But they were pestering them to buy the powerful BSAs and Triumphs from England and, increasingly, the quick, reliable Yamahas and Hondas from Japan. The kids had virtually no interest in the ancient German 3-horsepower oil burners that Harley dealers peddled.

Harley-Davidson lacked the technical expertise to develop a competitive, small-displacement bike. By the latter half of the 1950s, Harley did one thing: build large-displacement touring motorcycles—and they did it well, arguably better than anyone else at the time, but that ability did not automatically translate to the building of inexpensive, small-displacement, entry-level bikes. Harley had a serious problem on its hands. A decade earlier,

Harley had turned to Germany for a solution. Now it found itself under attack from Japan. To solve this new problem, it turned to the third major Axis power: Italy.

In the 1920s, the Italian company Aermacchi, short for "Aeronautica Macchi," built some of the world's most successful racing seaplanes. The company went on to build fighters for Mussolini's air force—at least until American bombers reduced the factory to rubble during World War II. After the war, Aermacchi dusted itself off and began building the small motorcycles that were desperately needed for transportation in postwar Italy. The range of well-designed two- and four-stroke models the company produced by the late 1950s seemed the ideal products with which Harley could counter the onslaught of small motorcycles from Asia. In 1960, Harley-Davidson bought 49 percent of Aermacchi for just $260,000 and began importing Aermacchi singles rebadged as Harley-Davidsons.

Harley brought over the Model C Sprint, a 250-cubic-centimeter four-stroke single, as its first Aermacchi-Harley hybrid. With 18 horsepower, the little Italian-

ducing the Rapido. Lo

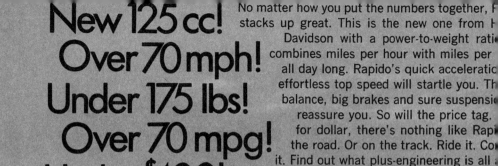

New 125 cc!
Over 70 mph!
Under 175 lbs!
Over 70 mpg!
Under $400!

No matter how you put the numbers together, F
stacks up great. This is the new one from H
Davidson with a power-to-weight rati
combines miles per hour with miles per
all day long. Rapido's quick acceleratio
effortless top speed will startle you. Th
balance, big brakes and sure suspensio
reassure you. So will the price tag.
for dollar, there's nothing like Rapi
the road. Or on the track. Ride it. Co
it. Find out what plus-engineering is all
Let Harley-Davidson put some fun ahead o
Rapido 125. At the Harley-Davidson dealer nea

Harley-Davidson
priced to meet competiti
+ engineered to beat

American could hit 70 miles per hour, making it more than a match for the early Hondas and Yamahas, though whether it lived up to the advertising hype is a matter of opinion. "Smartly styled in Calypso Red and White, this slim and trim beauty takes you out of the ordinary," period ad copy proclaimed, "takes you into a new world of motorcycling pleasure." The new Italians sold well, and by 1966, Harley was importing more than 20,000 Aermacchi two- and four-stroke motorcycles per year. While these numbers were good by traditional Harley standards, Japanese competitors were selling hundreds of thousands of motorcycles each year. Worse yet, they were branching out, building larger and larger motorcycles, to the point where they were encroaching on Harley's traditional large-displacement market.

The Aermacchi Harleys continued to sell relatively well into the mid-1970s, but by then Harley couldn't sell them nearly as fast as it was building them and was losing money on the venture. This was in part because of peculiarities in Italian labor laws, which allowed companies to decrease production but forbid laying off employees. If it was paying employees to build motorcycles, the company thought, they might as well build motorcycles, even if Harley couldn't actu-

ally sell all of the motorcycles those employees built.

The bikes began to stack up in show-rooms, then in warehouses around the world. Harley didn't even know where all the Aermacchi production was warehoused. Years later, they discovered warehouses full of unsold motorcycles in far-flung places like Brazil. Eventually, Harley decided it was throwing good money after bad; in June 1978, it closed the Aermacchi factory and sold the remaining assets to the Italian company Cagiva.

> "THE HARLEY-DAVIDSON TEAM WAS PERFECTLY SUITED TO [WALTER] VILLA . . . HIS TEAM LIKENED HIM TO A CATHOLIC PRIEST."
>
> FROM: "OBITUARY: WALTER VILLA" THE GUARDIAN, JULY 15, 2002

WILLIE G.

Once the Harley-Davidson Motor Co. was up and running as an industrial concern, Harley and the Davidson brothers blended into the background, focusing on the business of running a huge corporation rather than living in the public spotlight. Most fans would have been hard-pressed to name a single member of the family that retained ownership of the company during its first 60 years of operation. That all changed in the 1960s, when Willie G. Davidson, the grandson of company cofounder William A. Davidson, joined the company. Born in 1933, Willie G., as he is known to the Harley faithful, came of age in the post–World War II era and was steeped in the cultural zeitgeist of the time. His beatnik aesthetic is reflected in the ever-present beret atop his head, but more importantly his love of post-war custom motorcycles is present in every motorcycle he's had a hand in designing.

And he's designed or overseen the design of many, many motorcycles. After studying at the Art Center College of Design in Pasadena, California, Willie G. worked in the design department at Ford Motor Company before joining Harley's design department in 1963. Initially, Willie G.'s avant-garde esthetics were not well received by the hidebound executives then running the company. While corporate management didn't quite consist of cadavers, it's safe to assume that their flatus consisted of poofs of dust. Initially, the corporate oligarchs put him to work designing products they considered safe, like golf carts, but his flair for design on his early motorcycle projects—such as the 1966 Bobcat, which featured an innovative one-piece body that flowed from the gas tank to the rear fender—earned his superiors' respect. In 1969, he was promoted to Vice President of Design, a position he held for the next 33 years.

Willie G. was the right person at the right time. Harley desperately needed products that would resonate in the marketplace. Since World War II, the tastes of the Motor Company's customers had diverged completely from the aesthetic visions of Harley's design department. Riders wanted lithe, sleek, chopper-style motorcycles, and Harley was mostly building heavyweight, full-dress touring motorcycles, which Harley fans derided as "garbage wagons." If buyers did buy new Harley-Davidson big twins, they often stripped off all the accessories like windscreens and saddlebags—oftentimes along with the seats and fenders—mounted extended forks, and went off to recreate their own B-movie fantasies. Trouble was, they bought old Panheads or Knuckleheads to serve as canvases upon which to express their unique personalities far more often then they bought new machines, and Harley's new-bike sales plummeted.

When Willie G. took over Harley's design department, the first thing he did was create a bike that would fit the tastes of potential customers: the 1971 FX

1200 Super Glide. To create the anti-garbage wagon Super Glide, the design team stripped off all the accessories from a big twin touring bike and substituted the narrow fork from an XL Sportster for the wide-set fork used on the heavy touring models. The team developed a one-piece fiberglass seat-rear fender unit a bit like the one used on the smaller Bobcat, but this didn't resonate with customers and was soon replaced by a traditional seat and fender.

The fiberglass tailpiece might not have been a success, but the rest of the bike was, resulting in an entirely new class of motorcycle: the factory custom. With Willie G. at the helm

of Harley design, the company was in the perfect position to exploit the new genre, and a string of Willie G.-inspired successes followed: the 1977 FX Low Rider, the FXWG Wide Glide and FXB Sturgis (both from 1980), and a whole string of Softail models. These included the original 1984 FXST Softail, the 1986 Heritage Softail Classic, the 1988 FXSTS Springer, and the 1990 FLSTF Fatboy. There were misses, too, like the 1977 XLCR Café Racer and 1983-84 XR-1000, which featured high-performance bits from the company's all-conquering XR-750 racer, but even though these weren't successful when introduced, they've become highly collectible today.

Willie G. officially retired on April 30, 2012, ostensibly to pursue artistic pursuits like watercolor painting, but he still goes to the office every day, where he bears the title of Chief Styling Officer Emeritus and serves as the brand's ambassador.

BOATS, BOWLING BALLS, AND BICYCLES

"THE TEST OF THE MACHINE IS THE SATISFACTION IT GIVES YOU. THERE ISN'T ANY OTHER TEST. IF THE MACHINE PRODUCES TRANQUILITY IT'S RIGHT. IF IT DISTURBS YOU IT'S WRONG UNTIL EITHER THE MACHINE OR YOUR MIND IS CHANGED."

—ROBERT M. PIRSIG, *ZEN AND THE ART OF MOTORCYCLE MAINTENANCE: AN INQUIRY INTO VALUES*

In the 1960s, Harley-Davidson owned the large-displacement touring motorcycle category, and the company earned a profit selling such machines. That market was finite, though, with little room for growth, and Harley's stockholders wanted a better return on their investment. At that time, family members of the original founders only owned 53 percent of outstanding shares; the remaining 47 percent of the company was owned by investors who had bought stock in the company. The family members couldn't sell more stock or they would lose controlling interest in the company.

To increase profits, the company could diversify its product lineup and build refrigerators or washing machines, but Indian had attempted such diversification when motorcycle sales dried up after the advent of the Ford Model T, and the results had been less than successful. In fact Indian had ceased producing motorcycles in the United States in the early 1950s. There was little enthusiasm for emulating Indian's business plan at Harley's Milwaukee headquarters. The other option was to merge with a larger company, so Harley's president, William H. Davidson, began looking for someone to buy the company.

Why so many fleet owners make such a tidy profit with Harley-Davidson Golf Car Fleets

Sure, you won't see many golf cars at your local drive-in bank. But, you will see more fleet-owners of Harley-Davidson cars at the deposit window than of any other make. Harley-Davidson electric and gas powered golf cars stay on the course earning profits — stay out of the repair shop. Nearly 700 local Harley-Davidson servicing dealers are added assurance against costly down-time, and loss of rental-profits. Your profits are at stake if you fail to investigate Harley-Davidson before you buy one more golf car, or one more fleet. Phone your local Harley-Davidson dealer for a demonstration on your course, or write Sales Manager, Golf Car Division, Milwaukee, Wisconsin 53201.

EXCLUSIVE DYNA-START — Shuts off engine on gas car when foot is taken off accelerator. Starts engine when pedal is depressed. Eliminates gas-wasting idling.

EXCLUSIVE TWO-YEAR WARRANTY — Covers electric car's major components which are most susceptible to breakdown: solenoids, speed switch, resistor.

EXCLUSIVE AUTO-MATIC TRANSMIS-SION — Wheels can't spin and tear up the turf no matter how rapidly and far down accelerator pedal is depressed.

EXCLUSIVE SAFETY FEATURES — Wide-stance design and big 9.50 x 8 tires maintain stability whether you're driving up, down or across a steep incline.

Electric and Gasoline Golf Cars Engineered for Profitable Fleet Operation   **HARLEY-DAVIDSON**

Davidson discussed a possible sale with companies like Caterpillar, John Deere, OMC, and Chris-Craft, but by then Harley's assembly plant was filled with archaic manufacturing equipment and its production processes had changed little since World War I. Potential investors ran screaming when they realized the extent of the investment that would be required to modernize the company's facilities. The investors became increasingly impatient with Harley, and one stockholder finally contacted Bangor Punta (BP), a highly diversified company that built such varied products as Smith & Wesson guns, chemical mace, breathalyzers, motor homes, boats, and industrial machinery.

William H. Davidson and the board rejected BP's offer, so BP took its offer directly to the shareholders, offering them $32 per share, nearly 50 percent above market value. Davidson then approached American Machine & Foundry (AMF) and negotiated a sale for $29 per share. Founded in 1900 by Rufus L. Patterson, inventor of the first automated cigarette producing machine, the company had the sort of diversified portfolio that seemed to make Harley-Davidson a good fit, producing items like boats, bowling balls, and bicycles. BP countered with an offer of $40 per share, eventually upping that to $49 per share, but Harley's board stuck with AMF, and on January 8, 1969, Harley-Davidson Motor Company Inc. became AMF Harley-Davidson.

A SINKING SHIP

Willie G. Davidson's Super Glide had given Harley-Davidson's lineup a much-needed sales boost, but that didn't change the fact that, by the end of the 1970s, the company was in deep trouble, and AMF ownership was proving to be a mixed bag at best. AMF made President William H. Davidson chairman of the board, but, given that there was no board to chair, it really wasn't much of a promotion. AMF appointed John O'Brien president in his place. O'Brien came to Harley from Chrysler and had previously worked at Ford, but his background was in business and law, and he knew very little about the motorcycle market or motorcycles in general. O'Brien devoted few resources to product development. Instead, he focused on increasing production, believing that the best way to compete with the Japanese was building more bikes rather than building better bikes.

Given that Harley was building motorcycles that utilized 1930s technology—and building them in factories equipped with tooling that hadn't been updated since World War I—simply adding extra shifts and increasing output proved to be a less-than-satisfactory strategy. Output increased, but quality

control plummeted and before long AMF Harleys developed a terrible reputation for being unreliable. Instead of addressing quality concerns and updating the product, O'Brien's solution was to build even more antiquated, unreliable motorcycles at an unused AMF bowling equipment and munitions factory in York, Pennsylvania. Given that the Japanese competition had developed a reputation for rock-solid reliability, the Japanese began to eat Harley's lunch in the marketplace.

By 1975, the situation had become so disastrous that AMF finally agreed to spend money to develop two modern engines for Harley-Davidson motorcycles: the aluminum Evolution V-twin to replace the ancient cast-iron Shovelhead, and a stillborn liquid-cooled V-four, dubbed the "Nova," which never went into production (though the basic design was later used in the V-Rod V-twin engine). To keep customers interested in Harley's existing bikes, Willie G.'s styling department created exciting new models using the old engine. The resulting Low Rider, Fat Bob, Sturgis, and Wide Glide were still powered by a cast-iron boat anchor that predated the release of *Gone*

with the Wind, but they looked cool enough to get featured in enthusiast magazines and kept Harley's image alive.

On the downside, AMF continued to overproduce motorcycles, and reliability continued to suffer. In 1970, AMF's first full year of ownership, Harley's built just over 16,000 motorcycles in its US facilities. By 1976, AMF had tripled production to 48,000 units. As a result of the drastic decrease in quality and increased competition from Japan, Harley's share of the heavyweight motorcycle market fell from 75 percent in 1970 to around 35 percent in 1978. By 1980, AMF had had enough and was ready to rid itself of Harley-Davidson.

Harley Vice President Vaughn Beals conspired with top Harley executives and negotiated the sale of the company for $71 million with a down payment of just $1 million. On June 16, 1981, the investors became the proud owners of the last remaining American motorcycle company.

"ANYBODY CAN JUMP A MOTORCYCLE. THE TROUBLE BEGINS WHEN YOU TRY TO LAND IT."

—EVEL KNIEVEL

THE HARLEY-DAVIDSON TARIFF

> "LIFE SHOULD NOT BE A JOURNEY TO THE GRAVE WITH THE INTENTION OF ARRIVING SAFELY IN A PRETTY AND WELL PRESERVED BODY, BUT RATHER TO SKID IN BROADSIDE, IN A CLOUD OF SMOKE, THOROUGHLY USED UP, TOTALLY WORN OUT, AND LOUDLY PROCLAIMING, WOW! WHAT A RIDE!"
>
> — HUNTER S. THOMPSON

As the 1980s dawned, Japanese motorcycles dominated the market to such an extent that the older American and European manufacturers were endangered species. All the great British marques were dead or dying. Triumph, the one remaining mass producer of motorcycles in Britain in 1980, limped along for a few years before declaring bankruptcy in 1983. Germany's BMW fared a bit better because it had the backing of the company's automotive division, but even they suffered under the onslaught of cheap, fast, reliable motorcycles from Japan.

Harley-Davidson, America's sole remaining motorcycle manufacturer, was not in much better financial shape than its British rivals. Its heavyweight motorcycles still used an air-cooled, cast-iron, pushrod, two-valve V-twin that vibrated like a diesel-powered Soviet marital aid that couldn't compete against the reliable, fast, light, modern motorcycles that the Japanese produced. Harley had an advantage in sheer displacement—Harley's largest twin measured 1,340 cubic centimeters (80 cubic inches) while the biggest Japanese bikes in 1980 topped out at 1,100 cubic centimeters—but the high-tech Japanese bikes produced twice as much horsepower as the archaic Harleys. Things only got worse when Harley-Davidson found itself in the middle of a trade war, not between the Motor Company and its Japanese rivals, but between the Japanese rivals themselves. In an attempt to overtake perennial bestseller Honda, Yamaha flooded the US market with motorcycles. Honda responded in kind, and suddenly the US market exploded with Hondas and Yamahas. At the same time, the US economy plunged into a long, deep recession and motorcycle sales dried up, resulting in hundreds of thousands of unsold Yamahas and Hondas stacked up in warehouses across North America, which dealers blew out at prices 50 percent or more below retail. Bikes that cost $3,500 in 1982 were being advertised as carryover models priced at $1,600 by 1983.

Sales of Harley-Davidson's motorcycles, which cost between $4,500 and $7,000, plummeted. The glut of cut-price Japanese motorcycles on the market was nearly a coup de grâce for the fabled Milwaukee manufacturer. Harley reduced its production rate by half, laid off 40 percent of its workforce, and cut all salaries. On September 1, 1982, Chairman Vaughn Beals petitioned the International Trade Commission for relief. The ITC recommended tariffs of 45 percent on all Japanese motorcycles over 700cc and, on April 1, 1983, President Ronald Reagan signed the tariffs into law.

COASTING

The life Harley-Davidson has always been an exclusive life, one that appeals to people who view the world through a slightly different lens than do average citizens. Today, that exclusivity is a function of personal choices and values. A Harley rider values the freedom and mobility offered by a Harley more than the safety, comfort, and convenience offered by a Toyota Camry. A Harley rider values the visceral thrill of that big, loping V-twin engine over the 310 horsepower and 250-mile-per-hour top speed available from a Kawasaki H2R.

Prior to the introduction of Harley's Evolution engine, a more primitive factor made the life Harley-Davidson exclusive: the motorcycles themselves. Technological innovation defined the Motor Company during its first half century. When Harley introduced the magnificent Knucklehead for the 1936 model year, the world's first mass-produced superbike, it instantly made its side-valve competition obsolete. Boutique manufacturers like Crocker and Brough had manufactured powerful overhead-valve machines on a small scale, but these weren't available to the aver-

age rider. The Knucklehead offered the technology of the handcrafted high-performance specials for a fraction of the price.

The Knucklehead proved a technological high watermark for Harley-Davidson. Instead of building on the success of the Knucklehead, the Motor Company entered a decades-long coasting phase. In the years leading up to World War II, there was little need for anything more than fine-tuning the mighty Knuckle. It was the fastest, most powerful mass-produced motorcycle available in North America, the largest, richest market on earth. By 1936, Indian was on the ropes, its dated side-valve designs offering little competition for Harley's Knucklehead. In the years after the war, Europe focused on survival; European manufacturers produced crude little motorcycles to meet a desperate need for cheap transportation, leaving the market for big, powerful performance motorcycles exclusively to Harley.

As life returned to normal in postwar Europe, demand for more powerful and expensive motorcycles began to grow, and the European

manufacturers began building larger, more luxurious motorcycles. Harley made incremental improvements to the basic design of the Knucklehead, resulting in the Panhead of 1948. The company added hydraulic front forks in 1949 and, in 1957, it took the radical step of offering rear suspension. Since Indian had stopped producing proprietary motorcycles by that time, these small improvements should have been sufficient—but they weren't. In 1949, Triumph introduced a large-displacement (for the time) twin, the 650-cubic-centimeter Thunderbird 6T, and imported it to the United States. The Thunderbird produced 34 horsepower, compared to the 50 horsepower generated by the top Harley model, the 1,200-cubic-centimeter (74-cubic-inch) Panhead, but, out on the road, the much lighter and more nimble Triumph could keep up with the big Harley. Triumph began to cut into Harley sales, a trend that picked up speed when Marlon Brando rode a Thunderbird in the 1953 film *The Wild One*.

A NEAR-DEATH EXPERIENCE

The same year that Triumph brought the Thunderbird to the US market, Soichiro Honda began manufacturing a crude little two-stroke motorcycle in Japan. In 1958, Honda began exporting the Super Cub to the US market. At first this little oddity didn't seem like serious competition to the folks in Milwaukee, but they were tragically mistaken. Honda produced a string of increasingly larger and more sophisticated motorcycles like the 305-cubic-centimeter Dream, the CB450 twin, and finally the CB750 four-cylinder of 1969. While it gave away almost 500 cubic centimeters to Harley's biggest V-twin, the heavy, slow Shovelheads couldn't compete with the modern Honda. The Honda was cheaper, lighter, faster, and far more reliable. Anyone could afford these bikes, and anyone could ride them.

This marked the beginning of an onslaught of ever larger, ever more sophisticated, ever faster Japanese motorcycles. By the mid-1980s, Japan was producing liquid-cooled, high-performance superbikes that would be recognizable to any twenty-first-century rider, machines like the Kawasaki Ninjas, Honda Interceptors, and Suzuki GSX-Rs, which were faster than any supercar and as reliable as any Japanese sedan. Meanwhile, Harley was still producing slow, unreliable, cast-iron twins that leaked oil from every orifice and broke down so often and so completely that owning one required a rider with the ability to overhaul the engine at the side of a road on a moonless night with nothing but a Zippo lighter and an adjustable wrench.

RESURRECTION

This was Harley's darkest hour. At more than one point, the company was within hours of shutting down for good and joining all the other fabled marques on the scrap heap of history. But the folks running the company weren't ready to roll over and urinate on their soft underbellies in submission just yet. They had a new engine up their corporate sleeve: the Evolution. While still an air-cooled, pushrod V-twin, this was a thoroughly modern engine. It wasn't a technological powerhouse like the multivalve, multicylinder engines coming from Japan, but it didn't have to be; Harley understood its customers and their needs. Not everyone needed or wanted a motorcycle that could strafe apexes at 150 miles per hour. Many riders wanted a relaxed, character-laden American twin—which was, of course, what Harley had always produced, but previous generations had been too temperamental, crude, and, most importantly, too unreliable to tempt anyone but the most dedicated enthusiast away from Japanese and European motorcycles. The new Evolution was reliable, not as reli-

able as the liquid-cooled Japanese multis or even the remaining European motorcycles, but at least as reliable as that first Honda CB750 of 1969, and, for most people, that was reliable enough.

This completely kicked down all doors for Harley-Davidson. Americans loved Harleys. They loved the sound of them, and they loved the amazing styling coming from Willie G.'s design team. They had abandoned Harley-Davidson only because the motorcycles themselves had become thoroughly awful. With the introduction of the Evo, as it became known, Harleys went from being crude anachronisms to being genuine alternatives for motorcyclists seeking something different from the Japanese norm. Harley still built the most expensive motorcycle on the market—and, frankly still the slowest—but when the Motor Company added reliability to the mix, these slow, expensive, and exquisitely beautiful motorcycles began flying out of the showroom as fast as Harley could build them.

RICH URBAN BIKERS

These motorcycles were being sold to an entirely new breed of rider, someone who owned neither a Zippo lighter nor an adjustable wrench. Prior to the introduction of the Evo, Harley riders always looked dirty because they were covered with the oil that sprayed from their bikes. The grease from roadside repairs was so embedded in their fingernails that all the manicuring in the world couldn't get it out. That was the price one paid for entrance into the life Harley-Davidson. Suddenly that life was accessible to anyone who could ride a motorcycle and afford to buy a Harley. This meant that white-collar riders could join the blue-collar riders who comprised Harley's traditional customer base. That biker at the gas pump next to you was as likely to be a dentist or a corporate middle manager as he or she was to be a mechanic or a drug dealer.

The old-school Harley crowd resented this new breed. The old-timers considered the new riders effete elitists and gave them the derogatory name "rich urban bikers" ("rubbies"). Certainly many of these new riders weren't familiar with the customs and traditions of the life Harley-Davidson and many of the rubbies rubbed the old-timers the wrong way.

But the influx of rubbie money into Harley's corporate coffers didn't rub Harley's shareholders the wrong way. Sales of the new Evo-powered Harleys exploded. Soon Harley couldn't build enough motorcycles to meet the demand. People put their names on lists and waited months, even years for the privilege of buying new Harleys. The demand was so high that the price for used Harleys exceeded the price of new ones. The situation became downright ridiculous, with people buying new Harleys as

> "I HAVE THIS VINTAGE HARLEY-DAVIDSON MOTORCYCLE JACKET. WHEN I PUT IT ON, IT HAS THIS SUPERCOOL FEELING TO IT . . . "
>
> — ALICIA KEYS

speculative investments and selling them as soon as they arrived without ever riding them. This situation persisted into the early years of the twenty-first century, when production of new Harleys finally met the market's demand.

By this time, Harley had gone from being a struggling company producing antiquated products that only appealed to a handful of diehard outlaws to being the world's largest manufacturer of heavyweight motorcycles, a distinction it still holds today. Harley has continued to improve its motorcycles to keep pace with the market, and today its motorcycles are at least as good as those produced by its competition, and in many cases better. In today's more challenging consumer climate, building Harleys is not akin to printing money, as it was in the Motor Company's heyday, but Harley will always offer something that no other company can: the life Harley-Davidson.

"WE TRAVEL, SOME OF US FOREVER, TO SEEK OTHER STATES, OTHER LIVES, OTHER SOULS."

— ANAIS NIN

CHAPTER TWO

THE LIFE HARDWARE

PURE FILTH

The life Harley-Davidson defines those who choose to live it. It encompasses virtually every aspect of one's existence. And central to that life are the motorcycles themselves. Yes, they may just be machines, mechanical objects that serve the unglamorous function of hauling one's ass from point A to point B, but anyone who really believes that would not be reading this book. Some inanimate objects possess qualities that transcend their simple machine status. They have a quality of feel, of sound, of smell, a presence that defies the logical assumption that they are merely inanimate objects.

Take a guitar, for instance. A guitar is an assembly of wood and wire that should have no more character than, say, a power pole and a voltage line. But anyone who has ever bonded with a guitar knows this is not true. A good guitar has a voice, a spirit, a soul. When you hold a good guitar in your hands and begin to play, the bond between you and the guitar transcends anything that would be possible with a purely inanimate object.

Likewise, a motorcycle is just an assembly of mechanical parts: a motor, a fuel-storage container, some wheels and suspension bits to attach them to the motorcycle, a place for the rider to sit, and a frame to tie the whole thing together. This description could apply to a forklift, a golf cart, or even a lowly mobility scooter. But a motorcycle is much more than the sum of its parts. Like a good guitar, a good motorcycle communicates with its rider, not in words, but in action.

This is true of all motorcycles, but even though all hogs are created equal, some hogs are more equal than others. You have motorcycles and you have Harley-Davidsons. There is a difference. There are faster motorcycles, there are better-handling motorcycles, but few motorcycles communicate with their riders the way a Harley-Davidson does. Harleys have a presence that no other manufacturer has been able to capture.

The following is just a sampling of the great machines produced by Harley-Davidson over the past century-plus—there isn't space in this book to chronicle all of the Motor Company's offerings since 1903. If this selection doesn't ignite your lust for the life Harley-Davidson, you might want to consult your physician. James Joyce defined pornography as that which makes one desire to possess something. If Joyce was correct, grab some tissues, because we're about to embark on a journey of pure filth.

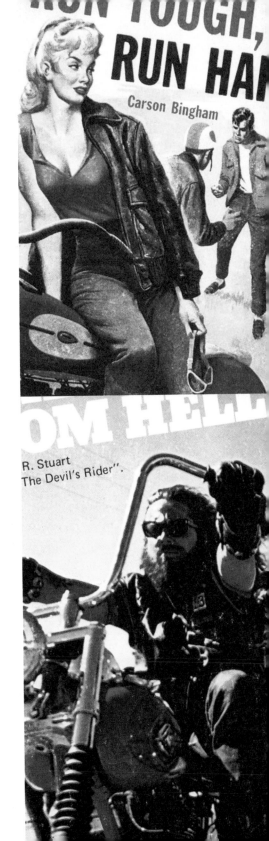

1903 SINGLE

The 1903 Harley-Davidson single, the motorcycle that bears serial number 1, is where the life Harley-Davidson began. Serial number 1, which resides in the Harley-Davidson Motor Co. Museum, features some components manufactured at a later date, but the bike is as correct as possible.

One feature that distinguished this Harley from its competitors was that it used a purpose-designed motorcycle frame, whereas most of Harley's competitors were producing motorized bicycles—literally bicycle frames with motors mounted in the V above the pedal cranks.

The first Harleys weren't really designed for mass production; rather, they were testbeds for experimentation, which probably explains the many changes that were made to serial number 1 over the first couple of years of its life. No one really knew what sort of market existed for a mass-produced motorcycle at the time, but when a machine was this well designed from the start, it's not surprising that Harley-Davidson developed a strong market.

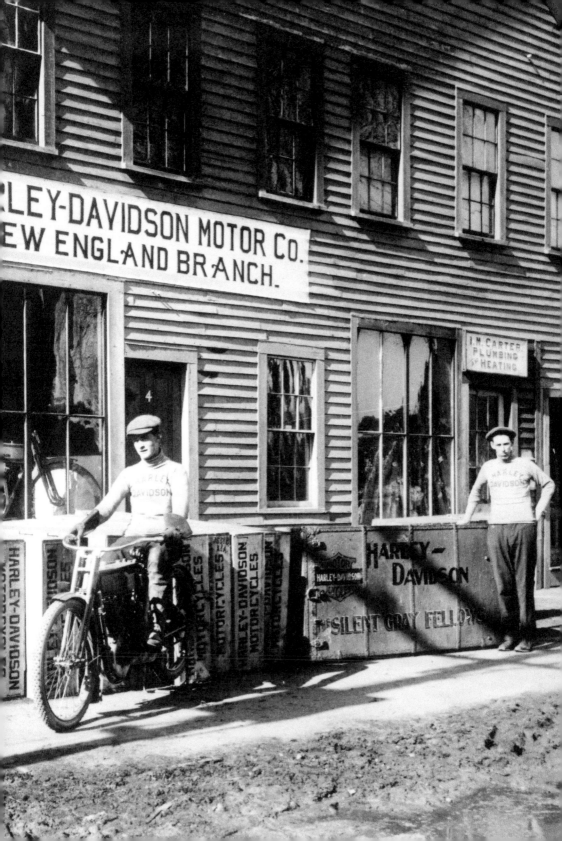

SILENT GRAY FELLOW

Anthropomorphizing Harley-Davidson motorcycles isn't a new phenomenon. Early on, Harley fans got in the habit of naming their machines. Because of the gray paint that graced most early Harleys, a Harley-Davidson motorcycle was often called a "Gray Fellow." By 1909, that name had found its way into official Harley promotional literature.

That year Harley introduced the Model 5, a new 30-cubic-inch single-cylinder engine that generated a whopping 4-plus horsepower. The Model 5 also featured an exhaust system that was so quiet that the nickname for the machine eventually became "Silent Gray Fellow." By 1912, Harley was making full use of this reputation for silence in its advertising:

Our claims that the Harley-Davidson is the cleanest, most silent, most comfortable, and the most economical motorcycle made, are rather broad, but can easily be verified. Its extreme cleanliness is due to the fact that all moving parts requiring oil are enclosed. As for silence, the Harley-Davidson is known everywhere as the "Silent Gray Fellow."

Today riders go to great lengths to make their Harleys as loud as possible, but in those early years, customers found quieter exhausts more appealing, and the Silent Gray Fellow was a sales success.

> "I FINALLY FELT MYSELF LIFTED DEFINITIVELY AWAY ON THE WINDS OF ADVENTURE TOWARD WORLDS I ENVISAGED WOULD BE STRANGER THAN THEY WERE, INTO SITUATIONS I IMAGINED WOULD BE MUCH MORE NORMAL THAN THEY TURNED OUT TO BE."
>
> —ERNESTO CHE GUEVARA, *THE MOTORCYCLE DIARIES*

MODEL J

Harley-Davidson's early experiments with V-twin engines didn't go well. In fact, its first production V-twin, the 1909 Model 5-D, was a complete disaster. The valve design, which had sufficed on the earlier singles, wasn't up to the task for the bigger twin-cylinder engine. Harley rectified that shortcoming and by 1912 was back in the big-displacement V-twin market with the Model 8-X-E. Then, as now, riders were hungry for more power, and the big-displacement V-twin models soon became Harley's bestselling machines.

By 1915, the largest V-twin model had evolved into the Model J, which would become the staple motorcycle in Harley's lineup for a generation. These were some of the fastest, most powerful, and best-built motorcycles available anywhere on the planet. It was on the strength of the various iterations of the Model J that Harley became the largest motorcycle manufacturer in America, and one of the largest in the world.

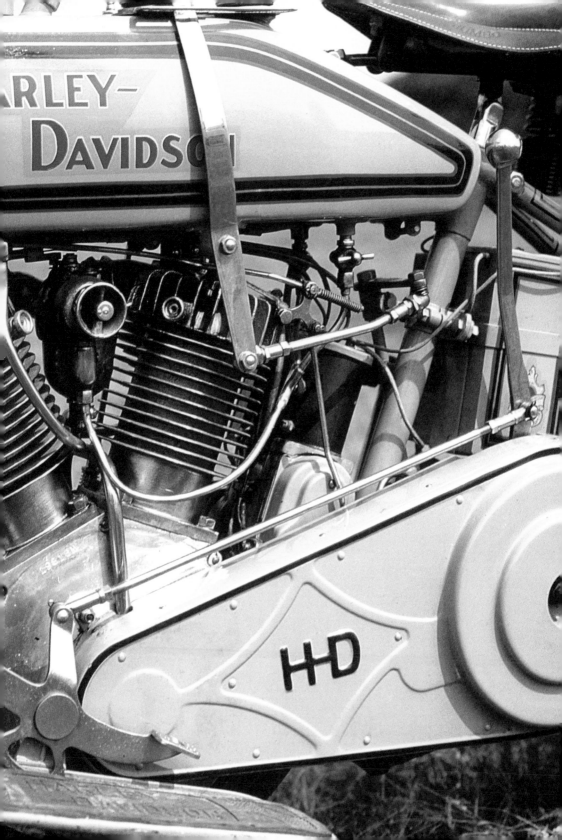

FLATHEADS

Harley-Davidson was relatively late in adopting side-valve heads ("flathead") to its engines, sticking with the De Dion-style intake-over-exhaust arrangement, which had been the dominant design in nineteenth-century internal combustion engines, long after most other manufacturers had abandoned the design in favor of the flathead engine.

Today we think of the flathead as a relic from another era, something only used today because it looks cool in a period-correct '32 Ford hot rod; in the early years of the twentieth century, it was the premier performance engine. The fuels available during the period contained lower octane ratings than the urine of a high-functioning alcoholic, and, with gasoline that can be legitimately compared to piss, the flathead pro-duces more power than does an overhead valve engine.

Harley's first flathead wasn't a traditional V-twin, or even a conventional single, but rather the Weird Harold Model 20-W Sport of 1919. An opposed twin-cylinder engine, much like the boxer-type engine powering today's BMW motorcycles, except mounted longitudinally in the frame, powered the Model W Sport.

Harley went on to produce a line of successful models powered by flathead engines. Ultimately, the flat head design was made obsolete by one of Harley's all-time great motorcycles—the Knucklehead—along with the introduction of tetraethyl lead in gasoline that enabled octane ratings to sky-rocket, but, for a series of strange reasons, Harley continued to pro-duce flathead-powered motorcy-cles into the 1970s.

The longevity of the flathead was partly due to Harley bullying the American Motorcyclist's Association (AMA) into instituting racing rules that gave American flathead-powered motorcycles an advantage over the overhead

> "HALF THE FUN OF THE TRAVEL IS THE AESTHETIC OF LOSTNESS."
> — RAY BRADBURY

valve competition from Europe. This in turn forced Harley to produce flathead-powered motorcycles long after there was any market for such archaic machines.

In 1952, Harley brought out its first all-new motorcycle since the 1936 Knucklehead: the Model K. Although this was a modern motorcycle in most respects, its 45-cubic-inch V-twin engine retained the side-valve design to comply with AMA racing rules. Harley had boxed itself into a corner with its AMA rules manipulation and was forced to produce a motorcycle no one wanted. The Model K was quickly abandoned for a much more successful overhead-valve model, the Model XL Sportster.

That wasn't the end of the line for the venerable flathead engine: in 1932, Harley had introduced a strange three-wheeled vehicle for industrial use called the "Servi-Car." This contraption was powered by a 45-cubic-inch flathead engine. The Servi-Car proved popular with police departments around the United States, who assigned it to meter maids. Harley continued to strike terror into the hearts of parking scofflaws with its peculiar three-wheeled flathead until production ceased in 1973.

KNUCKLEHEAD

Without a doubt, the most influential model in Harley-Davidson's history was the 1936 Model E, which featured Harley-Davidson's first 61-cubic-inch overhead-valve V-twin engine as its party piece. Nicknamed the "Knucklehead" because of the rounded shapes of the rocker covers—which resembled a closed hand, knuckles up—the astounding new engine produced a claimed 40 horsepower. For just $380, a buyer got a genuine superbike, one of the fastest vehicles available anywhere. Though the bike itself was beautiful—to this day custom motorcycle builders work to emulate the Knucklehead's graceful lines—the most significant aspect of the machine was its powerful overhead-valve V-twin engine. Harley knew it had something special on its hands, as illustrated in the flowery language of period advertising:

> *Minus fanfare and ballyhoo, a new motorcycle has come on the scene and has taken the world by storm . . . As one owner writes, "It's my dream come true . . ." Its wonderful handling qualities, its snappy response, its ability to stand up and "take it" make this 61 OHV the outstanding motorcycle of today and the motorcycle of tomorrow.*

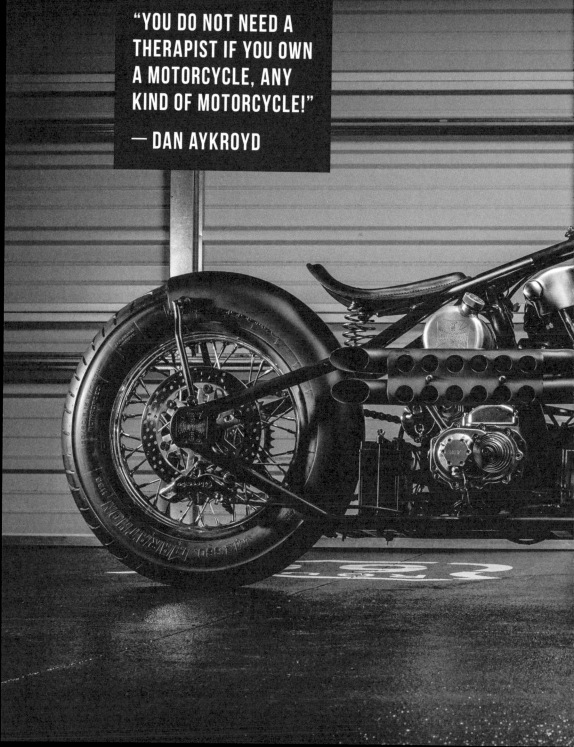

"YOU DO NOT NEED A THERAPIST IF YOU OWN A MOTORCYCLE, ANY KIND OF MOTORCYCLE!"

— DAN AYKROYD

1942 MODEL WLA

Though the Jeep soon replaced the motorcycle as the preferred vehicle for carrying troops in and out of battle and for military courier service, the Jeep was not available at the dawn of World War II, and the US military bought Harley-Davidson's Model WLA by the tens of thousands.

All WLA models manufactured during the war were labeled as 1942 models regardless of their year of manufacture, though the WLA was manufactured for military use as late as 1952. The Motor Company built a total of 61,101 WLA models in military and civilian specification during that period, as well as another 17,823 WLC models designed for use with sidecars. As important as motorcycle sales were to Harley's bottom line, the contract that the military negotiated with Harley likely meant that the Motor Company didn't earn much profit from each unit sold.

PANHEAD

In 1948, Harley-Davidson updated the Knucklehead powerplant, incorporating aluminum cylinder heads, hydraulic valve lifters, and chrome-plated, pan-shaped rocker-arm covers that inspired the nickname: Panhead.

In 1949, the Motor Company introduced a new front suspension that featured a hydraulic fork in place of the ancient springer setup and dubbed the updated machine "Hydra-Glide." The rest of the motorcycling world had long ago switched to hydraulic front forks, most importantly the British bikes, which had begun to cannibalize Harley-Davidson sales, but that didn't stop Harley from touting this feature everyone else took for granted:

> "SOMETIMES IT'S A LITTLE BETTER TO TRAVEL THAN TO ARRIVE"
>
> — ROBERT M. PIRSIG, *ZEN AND THE ART OF MOTORCYCLE MAINTENANCE*

For the grandest vacation you ever had, swing into the saddle of a Hydra-Glide Harley-Davidson . . . . You'll ride all day and, if you wish, far into the night and still feel like going on and on . . . You'll glide over endless tar lines and over rough spots. You'll hit bumpy side roads and country lanes with barely a quiver. Gone is that feeling of fatigue. After a day of hundreds of miles of travel, you'll wake up the next morning fresh as a daisy—eager to get going and see more of this great country of ours.

While buyers appreciated the improved suspension, they increasingly expected more from their motorcycles. Riders were becoming used to the modern features found on imported machines, but Harley had become a notoriously stodgy company, reluctant to adopt the modern features found on most imported motorcycles. For example, Harley didn't introduce a foot-shifted transmission on big twin models until the 1952 model year.

Worse yet, Harley-Davidson kept using the archaic rigid frame on its biggest machines until the 1958 model year, when it finally introduced the Duo-Glide, a big twin with swinging-arm rear suspension. And it wasn't until the advent of the 1965 Electra-Glide that Harley finally offered electric starting on its most expensive motorcycles.

Throughout this period, Harley had been losing market share. First the Brits made inroads, and then Japanese motorcycles hit the American market like an atomic bomb, with affordable prices, unheard-of convenience features like electric starting, and unprecedented reliability. As a result, the Panhead's sales declined throughout its lifecycle. When Harley introduced the Panhead in 1948, it sold 8,071 units. By 1965, the last year of Panhead production, the Motor Company sold just 4,800 units.

SPORTSTER

The earlier Model K had fulfilled its primary mission—provide a platform that would dominate AMA racing—but because AMA rules favored the antiquated flathead engine design, the street version of the Model K was hampered with that side-valve lump of an engine, and its sales suffered mightily.

In 1957, Harley-Davidson rectified the situation and introduced the Model XL Sportster with a 55-cubic-inch overhead-valve engine. The Sportster suffered from being rushed to market. For example, the modern aluminum cylinder heads of the Model K were abandoned for crude cast-iron cylinder heads like those found on the 1936 Knucklehead.

Because money was tight, Harley lifted the basic frame and running gear from the Model K. That wasn't necessarily a bad thing; other than its flathead engine, the Model K was a relatively modern motorcycle that featured an integral four-speed, foot-shifted transmission, a telescopic front fork, and swinging-arm rear suspension.

These first Sportsters were criticized for being slow, primarily because the cast-iron cylinder heads hadn't been properly developed. The 1959 Sportsters received larger valves and compression was bumped. The hottest version—the XLCH—was one of the fastest motorcycles sold in America.

The Sportster's supremacy was short-lived. By the late 1960s, the Japanese were selling large-displacement motorcycles that made the Sportster look like the relic it was. In 1973, Harley bumped displacement to 1,000 cubic centimeters and for one year only dropped the Sportster name, giving the bike the more exotic-sounding name "XL1000," but by then the Japanese were importing modern four-cylinder superbikes. A name change and another 100 cubic centimeters of displacement weren't enough to make a bike with 1936 technology competitive against a Kawasaki Z-1.

On the styling front, the Sportster was more competitive. The old beast might have been a slow lump of cast iron, but at least it looked good going slow. Harley even took on the Europeans in styling; in 1977, Willie G. Davidson's design team brought out the stunning 1000 Café Racer.

"YESTERDAY'S WEIRDNESS IS TOMORROW'S REASON WHY."

— HUNTER S. THOMPSON,
THE CURSE OF LONO

By 1983, the Sportster had become a joke, as had the Harley-Davidson Motor Company itself. The company was barely in business and few people expected it to survive. Even Harley employees expected the doors to shut at any time. The last great old-school Sportster model—the XR-1000—was built as much to boost employee morale as it was to produce a motorcycle for public consumption.

Because there was no money for research and development (there was barely enough money to keep the lights on), Harley raided its parts bin to produce the XR-1000, a hybrid that mounted the aluminum racing heads and twin Dell'Orto slide-valve carburetors from the XR-750 race bike on an XL-1000 Sportster's engine.

The cobbled-together nature of this machine was evident to anyone who tried to ride one—the engine ran so rough that it sounded like it had marbles in its crankcase—but the bike fulfilled its primary purpose: to let the world (and Harley employees) know that the Motor Company wasn't dead yet. The day the first XR-1000 rolled off the assembly line, the first really new Sportster in decades, Harley employees stopped what they were doing and cheered.

BUELL BATTLETWIN

The year 1985 marked the end of the line for the original cast-iron XL engine, which had remained essentially unchanged for the better part of three decades. The 1985 XLH-1000 Sportster was the last mass-produced motorcycle manufactured in the Western world that still used cast-iron cylinder barrels and cylinder heads. The following year, Harley introduced a new line of Sportsters that featured modern aluminum engines based on the Evolution big twins introduced in 1984.

But the cast-iron 1930s technology would live on in the Buell RR-1000 Battletwin. A national AMA road racer and a chassis engineer for Harley-Davidson, Erik Buell left Harley in 1982 to build his own racing motorcycles. In 1985, Buell built a series of bikes using leftover Harley XR-1000 engines mated to his own racing chassis. By the time production ended in 1987, Buell had produced 50 of his RR-1000 models.

SHOVELHEAD

While Harley-Davidson had been handed its ass in the lightweight and middleweight displacement classes, first by the British and then by the Japanese, in the mid-1960s it still owned the heavyweight touring bike market. While the family members still controlling the company purse strings were notoriously tight—some say that only dogs could hear their flatus expulsions—they had the sense to invest in developing the big twin engines powering their most profitable bikes. In 1966, Harley introduced an updated big twin.

As had been tradition since before World War II, the new engine's nickname was based on the appearance of its cylinder heads. In this case, the new engine was called the "Shovelhead," though the resemblance to any sort of shovel is tenuous at best. Perhaps the person who coined the nickname was nearsighted and had consumed large quantities of alcohol.

Be that as it may, the new engine's most notable new features were its distinctive cylinder heads, which offered marginally improved top-end oiling. In 1969, Harley abandoned the old-fashioned generator electrical system and replaced it with a more modern alternator. This altered the look of the bottom end of the engine substantially. The post-1969 Shovelheads are often called "cone Shovels" because the alternator sat behind a pointy, cone-shaped cover at the end of the crankshaft.

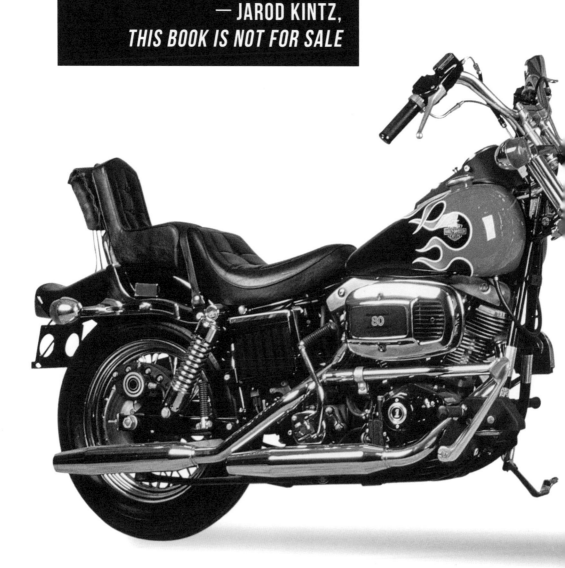

"I THINK THE BEST TIME TO STARE
OFF INTO SPACE IS WHEN YOU'RE
GOING 65 ON A MOTORCYCLE,
PROVIDED YOU'RE WEARING YOUR
ASTRONAUT'S HELMET."

— JAROD KINTZ,
THIS BOOK IS NOT FOR SALE

FACTORY CUSTOMS

The Shovelhead received only minor improvements throughout its life. By the time it was retired for good after the 1984 model (a small number of 1985 models equipped with leftover Shovelhead engines were sold to US police departments), the Shovelhead engine was nearly as antiquated as the old iron-head Sportster engine. Styling, though, was one area where the Shovelhead models continued to dominate.

This stylistic ascendance began in 1971, when Harley introduced the FX Super Glide. While featuring technology that other manufacturers had abandoned decades earlier, the

Super Glide's styling was so spot-on for the time that it kept Harley-Davidson afloat throughout the following decade.

The motorcycle market had experienced dramatic changes in the late 1960s and early 1970s as the baby boom generation came of age and began buying motorcycles by the millions. These younger buyers mostly bought the fast, reliable, and inexpensive motorcycles coming from Japan, but a certain percentage of young people were more interested in the customized motorcycles shown in films like *Easy Rider* than they were in either the Japanese superbikes or the slow, heavyweight touring bikes that Harley-Davidson produced. These new buyers demanded a new style of motorcycle, and that's just what Willie G. Davidson gave them. Davidson's styling department mated a big twin chassis to a Sportster front end to create the Super Glide. It proved to be exactly what the market wanted: Harley sold 4,700 Super Glides in the first year of production.

In 1977, Harley took the factory custom motorcycle one step further and introduced the FXS-1200 Low Rider, with an extended fork, a drag-

style handlebar on a 3.5-inch riser, cast wheels, and black-and-silver engine with painted side covers. But Harley's design department didn't stop there; in 1980, it brought out two customs that made the Low Rider seem tame by comparison.

The first, the FXB-80 Sturgis, was an extraordinarily black machine with orange accents. It was named after the infamous annual motorcycle rally held in the Black Hills of South Dakota each August. This technologically interesting motorcycle abandoned both the primary drive chain and final drive chain, replacing both with belt-drive systems. The primary belt system never really caught on, but the belt final-drive system did; today it's used on every motorcycle that Harley builds.

The second radical custom, the FXWG-80 Wide Glide, was less revolutionary from a technological standpoint but featured even wilder styling. With its bobtail rear fender, forward foot controls, wide front fork with extended tubes, flamed five-gallon gas tank, and staggered shorty exhausts, the Wide Glide came closer to replicating the look of the radical custom chopper than had any previous factory custom.

EVOLUTION

For the 1984 model year, Harley-Davidson introduced the single most important product in its long history: the all-new 1340cc Evolution engine. With aluminum heads and aluminum cylinders with cast-iron inner liners, the Evolution engine literally saved the company. In many ways, the engine represented state-of-the-art Japanese technology circa 1967; really, that was no bad thing.

By 1984, Japan Incorporated was producing 100-plus horsepower, liquid-cooled, multicylinder rocket bikes with which Harley's pushrod V-twin could not hope to compete. But Harley-Davidson motorcycles didn't need to compete with those racers for the street; all they really had to do was be reliable enough to conform to modern standards—and, more importantly, look good while doing so. People loved Harley's styling. They lusted after it, but the antique cast-iron engines powering that styling were too unreliable for people to take the plunge and buy Harley-Davidson motorcycles.

With the introduction of the Evolution engine, that situation changed overnight. The Evo made Harleys accessible to anyone

who wanted one. Now people who longed for motorcycles that looked like Harleys had no reason not to buy real Harleys.

The new engine might have been the big news, but Harley wasn't resting on its laurels when it came to styling. The same year that Harley introduced the Evolution engine, it brought out its most radical custom to date: the 1984 FXST Softail. The Softail emulated the classic lines of earlier motorcycles with no rear suspension—the hard tails—but featured a modern rear suspension cleverly hidden beneath the transmission. The classically styled Softail, with its modern-ish engine and suspension, was a recipe that combined everything many people wanted in a motorcycle; the new Evo-powered Softail was a hit. Harley sold 5,413 examples in 1984.

Two years later, Harley doubled down on the nostalgia factor and introduced the FLST Heritage Softail, a Softail styled to look almost exactly like a 1949 Hydra-Glide. The Heritage Softail had all the period-correct bits needed to make any fan of American motorcycles go a big rubbery one:

fender tip lights, front running lights, a pleated seat, heel-and-toe-shifter, and floorboards.

In 1989, Harley dug even deeper into its storied past and produced the FXSTS Springer Softail, which revived the springer front end that Harley hadn't offered since 1952. While the springer front fork technology had been abandoned during Harry S. Truman's presidency, springers remained popular among custom bike builders and Harley had another success on its hands.

The following year, Harley dropped its own atomic bomb on the motorcycle market: the 1990 FLSTF Fat Boy. Though Willie G. Davidson remains coy about the subject to this day, the name has long been rumored to be a cross between "Fat Man" and "Little Boy," the names given the atomic bombs that the US dropped on Japan in 1945.

To create the Fat Boy, Harley-Davidson started with a Heritage Softail and added monochromatic silver paint. First-year Fat Boys featured Uranium Yellow highlights on the timer and derby covers and on the center rocker-box spacers.

In the film *Terminator 2: Judgment Day*, Arnold Schwarzenegger spends half of his on-screen time rampaging aboard a Fat Boy, turning the film into the best motorcycle advertisement ever made. Not that Harley needed the publicity— Evolution-powered Harleys were wildly successful without it. In 1983, the year before the Evolution engine hit the market, Harley sold 29,500 motorcycles. In 1999, the last year of regular production for the Evolution engine, that number had risen to 184,954.

"I NEED YOUR CLOTHES, YOUR BOOTS, AND YOUR MOTORCYCLE"

— ARNOLD SCHWARZENEGGER, *TERMINATOR 2 JUDGEMENT DAY*

TWIN CAM

In 1999, Harley brought out another new engine design, the Twin Cam 88, followed a year later by a counterbalanced version of the engine called the Twin Cam 88B. This 1,450-cubic-centimeter V-twin abandoned the cone-shaped bottom end that had been in use since 1969 for a redesigned bottom end that featured two cams instead of one.

The 88B version featured a counter balancer that greatly reduced engine vibration. This was used in the Softail models, which still mounted the engines solidly to the frames rather than in vibration-isolating rubber mounts, as was done on other big twins. (Sportster models would get rubber mounts for the 2004 model year).

Using solid rather than rubber motor mounts allowed Softail models to retain their slim-waisted good looks—by contrast, the models with rubber-mounted engines looked like they'd eaten one too many ammonia-soaked anus-and-eyeball burgers at McDonald's—but this also made the motorcycles vibrate like jackhammers. The counter balancer made the Softail models as smooth as the touring models.

As the new century got underway, Harley seemed to focus most of its efforts on the lucrative luxury market. The company's Custom Vehicle Operations (CVO) raided Harley's "Screamin' Eagle" parts catalogs for every chrome and luxury bit it could find, slapped on some flashy paint, and sold the finished products for as much money as the market would allow. A 2004 FLHTCSE Screamin' Eagle Electra Glide sold new for $29,000, and the prices would only go up from there. By the time the last Twin Cam-powered CVO Limited model rolled off the line for the 2016 model year, the price had hit $39,999.

MILWAUKEE 8

For the 2017 model year, Harley-Davidson introduced another new big twin. This was just the sixth new big twin in the 81 years since the debut of the original Knucklehead, so it was a momentous occasion. The engine came in two sizes: 107 cubic inches (1,750 cubic centimeters) or 114 cubic inches (1,870 cubic centimeters). For 2017, only the big touring models received the new engines, but, like the Twin Cam before it, the Milwaukee 8, as it was officially called, would soon spread to the rest of the line.

The larger version of the engine featured liquid-cooled cylinder heads. This version was used on Ultra Limited, Road Glide Ultra, and Tri Glide models, which had fairing lowers, providing convenient locations for hiding unsightly radiators and associated plumbing. The models without fairing lowers made do without liquid cooling. Harley-Davidson owners tend to be traditionalists; they prefer the look of an air-cooled engine, but excessive engine heat has long been a complaint among Harley owners, particularly as engine displacement

became ridiculously huge. Hiding the radiator solved the heating problem without harming that prized air-cooled look.

The "8" in the name refers to the number of valves found in the new cylinder heads. In addition to being more efficient than two-valve designs, four-valve-per-cylinder heads run cooler, further alleviating the heat problem. Additional benefits include more power and better fuel economy.

The Milwaukee 8 abandoned the two-cam arrangement that gave the Twin Cam its name for a quieter, more reliable single-cam arrangement. Company engineers also gave the new engine a counterbalancer similar to the one used on the B version of the Twin Cam engine. This marked the company's first use of a counterbalancer on a rubber-mounted engine. Engineers deliberately tuned in some vibration, because market research showed that buyers want their Harleys to vibrate a little, but not enough to shake apart engine components or give passengers happy endings.

CUSTOMS

As long as companies have been building stock motorcycles, motorcyclists have been modifying stock motorcycles to make them better suited for their particular needs. We can trace custom motorcycles at least back to 1902, when a British engineer named Harold "Oily" Karslake took bits and pieces from several different motorcycles and built a bike he called the "Dreadnought."

Old Oily might have been one of the first motorcyclists to build a custom bike, but he was far from the last. Motorcyclists, it seems, cannot leave well enough alone, and Harley riders are the worst of the lot when it comes to modifying their machines.

Over the years, many custom bike styles have come and gone, then come and gone again. The following list contains some of the most common types of customs you'll likely encounter today.

117

BOBBER

In the early years of motorcycling, there was no aftermarket industry manufacturing virtually any custom part or motorcycle decoration one could possibly imagine; today, there is no limit to what you can order online. Do you want to make your Harley look like dragon from a fantasy film? No problem—go online and you'll find several Fiberglas dragon-head kits to mount to your motorcycle. Do you want to turn your hog into a 1959 Cadillac hearse, complete with black tail fins and a built-in stripper pole? Again, no problem. Type whatever peculiarity comes to mind into Google and within milliseconds you'll have dozens of vendors willing to sell you the most outlandish parts conceivable.

This was not the case in the early years of motorcycling. Long after Oily built his Dreadnought, the only way to get custom motorcycle parts was to make them yourself. This required a high level of machining skills and specialized tools like lathes, drills, welders, and torches. Removing parts to lighten the bike, thus improving handling and acceleration, was far easier, so this became the preferred form of customization. The earliest style of custom was known as the "cut down," because owners simply cut off and removed any parts not needed for the job at hand.

In America, the preferred motorcycle for building a cut down was Harley-Davidson's Model J. Cut down Model Js proved so popular that the AMA introduced a new class of racing just for cut down stock motorcycles. Non racers liked the looks of these machines and began to copy the style for their street bikes, resulting in the bob job, or bobber.

The defining characteristic of a bobber is minimalism. Bobbers usually don't feature anything that isn't absolutely necessary, such as mirrors, turn signals primary covers, or even fenders. Bobbers were the earliest common street customs and remain popular to this day.

THERE ARE NO
SHORTCUTS
TO ANY PLACE
WORTH GOING.

—BEVERLY SILLS

CHOPPER

In the 1950s a new, more radical breed of custom Harley-Davidson began to appear. Motorcycle drag racing was becoming popular, requiring specialized motorcycles: bikes that were modified to go in a straight line rather than carve through a corner. The resulting bikes were long and low, with radically raked and lengthened forks, larger wheels, and small fuel tanks.

Early on, drag racers—both on two-wheels and four—discovered that flashy paint jobs and lots of chrome won them as many fans as winning races, so drag bikes were usually adorned with flashy paint and shiny chrome in equal measure. As always seems to be the case, fans of motorcycle drag racing began modifying their own motorcycles to resemble the flamboyant race bikes they watched at local drag strips.

This style of custom first became popular on the American West Coast. The bikes that most closely resembled drag racers were called "diggers," but these soon evolved into what we now think of as choppers. The chopper became the preeminent type of American custom in the 1960s, and, like everything else that appeared in that decade of excess, they became increasingly outrageous as the years went on. Forks got longer, apehanger handlebars got more apelike, and sissy bars stretched to the sky.

The chopper-style custom seems to wax and wane in popularity, usually following the same trajectory. At first, someone will build a tasteful chopper that captures riders' imaginations. Then more and more people build choppers, starting a movement. As the choppers become increasingly popular, builders will go to more and more outlandish lengths trying to capture the public's imagination. Eventually the trend hits its zenith, but builders still continue to build increasingly bizarre choppers until no one can stand the sight of them anymore. Then the trend will go dormant for a generation, until a new breed of young builder starts experimenting with chopper-style customs again and starts the whole cycle over.

CAFÉ RACER

124

> "ON MY TOMBSTONE THEY WILL CARVE, IT NEVER GOT FAST ENOUGH FOR ME."
>
> —HUNTER S. THOMPSON, *KINGDOM OF FEAR*

Another popular style of custom hearkens back to the earliest cut-downs and bob-jobs, but with a different aesthetic. Like those earlier bikes, café racers are customized, at least to some degree, for performance as well as appearance. Café racers originated in the United Kingdom and reflect a more European approach to motor-cycling. Just as American-style customs reflect American-style racing, café racers reflect European-style racing.

In the US, motorcycle racing evolved from horseracing, where horses raced around dirt-covered oval tracks. American motorcyclists began racing their motorcycles on horse tracks; as a result, the preeminent form of American motorcycle racing throughout the twentieth century was known as "dirt-track" racing, competitions in which motorcycles raced each other around dirt-covered oval tracks that often doubled as horseracing tracks. This resulted in a specific type of racing motorcycle, one designed not so much for agility but for stability in difficult conditions. And one that looked very much like a cutdown or bob-job.

In Europe, road racing—competing on twisting paved circuits—was the preeminent form of motorcycle racing, and the machines used in competition had to be agile and able to change direction quickly. This required its own specific form of customization: fairings to cut the wind at high speeds, low, clip-on handlebars, and rearset footpegs to put the riders in position to control their machines. This is the style that evolved into the café racer.

The term "café racer" came into common usage after World War II, when the children born during and after the war became old enough to ride motorcycles. These younger riders would often meet up at cafes. Being young (usually) men with more

testosterone than common sense, these young riders would go out and race from café to café on public roads, resulting in the name that described both the riders and the machines they rode.

The holy grail for the café racers was to "do the ton"—that is, reach 100 miles per hour on public roads. Given that these were young men with limited funds, they usually couldn't afford to buy the latest, greatest motorcycles that could easily top 100 miles per hour, so they modified the motorcycles they could afford in an attempt to do the ton.

In the early years, café racers were primarily a European phenomenon, just as bobbers and choppers were primarily found in America. In fact, café racers were so foreign in the US market that, when Harley-Davidson produced its lovely XLCR café racer in 1977, the bike was a sales flop. Over the years, though, the lines blurred. Bobbers and choppers began to appear in Europe and café racers became increasingly popular in the US.

Traditionally, café racers have been based on European and Japanese motorcycles, but the style is becoming increasingly popular among Harley riders, too. Somewhere along the line, people discovered that Harleys make excellent café racers, particularly Harley Sportsters.

CHAPTER THREE

THE LIFE
MOTORCYCLE CLUB

> "THE STORY OFF THE HELLS ANGELS MOTORCYCLE CLUB IS THE STORY OF A VERY SELECT BROTHERHOOD OF MEN WHO WILL FIGHT AND DIE FOR EACH OTHER, NO MATTER WHAT THE CAUSE."
>
> —SONNY BARGER
> HELLS ANGEL

Harley-Davidson builds some of the most desirable vehicles on earth, but there's a lot more to the Life Harley-Davidson than just the machines. When you become a Harley rider, you become more than just a motorcyclist. You become a member of the club.

The life Harley-Davidson is a life lived as part of a community, an extended family of riders bonded by their love of the lifestyle as much as of the bikes themselves. Author and *Easyriders* editor-in-chief Dave Nichols calls it becoming a member of "the tribe."

Sonny Barger of Hells Angels fame takes it one step farther. Barger describes being part of the motorcycling community as a religious experience: "For me, riding a motorcycle is like being part of a ceremony; it's something holy. I think a lot of my club brothers feel the same way. That's why we call going to our club meetings 'going to church.'"

The sense of community isn't just limited to Harley riders; as soon as you start riding any motorcycle, you'll find that you're part of a larger community of motorcycle riders. When you first encounter the rider wave—motorcycle riders waving at one another when they meet on a road—you'll notice that they wave regardless of what you're riding. It doesn't matter if the other rider is some kid on a sport bike, an adventure-tourer traveling the globe on a big dual-sport bike, or a member of a one-percenter club; riders wave at one another as a way of acknowledging that we're all in this together.

Waving goes back to the early days of riding. Back then, bikes were so unreliable that traveling to the next town down the road was considered a big trip; a rider had to know how to fix a bike to ride it. You needed more than just a fat wallet to become a biker, because, in the old days, a rider spent as spent as much time working on a bike as riding it. Every time a person went for a ride on a motorcycle, there was a fair chance something would go wrong before he or she returned home.

Today, motorcycles are much more reliable and everyone has a cell phone; on the odd chance that something does go wrong, a rider can just call for help. In the old days, when a bike (inevitably) broke down, a rider had two choices: fix it or walk to the nearest telephone.

This notorious unreliability kept most people from joining the motorcycle community, which made motorcycling more or less a blue-collar activity. This created a class-based division between riders and non riders that would last for many generations—and it fostered a sense of brotherhood among riders.

In part, this brotherhood came about as the result of the antimotorcycle hysteria that infected the United States in the years after World War II, which we'll discuss in more detail in chapter 4. With

Communism spreading around the world and the Soviet Union getting an atomic bomb, people were scared of anything out of the ordinary, and in those days riding a motorcycle was definitely out of the ordinary. If a rider was lucky, he or she might see one other motorcycle on an entire trip. This was such an exciting occurrence that the riders automatically waved at one another. They might even pull over at the nearest roadhouse and share a refreshing beverage.

Not that they'd be accepted in most roadhouses: after the release of *The Wild One*, antimotorcycle hysteria reached a fever pitch. In his book, *Let's Ride*, Sonny Barger describes his first encounter this antimotorcycle prejudice:

In 1958, I was hanging out at a doggy diner on Twenty-third Avenue. I'd just been fired from my job and was sitting out in front of the diner when a straight-laced cop pulled up and told me that he'd been down to visit my boss the day before. I realized that he'd been the person who'd gotten me fired. From that day forward, it's gotten progressively worse. Just a couple of days ago I got a speeding ticket; the Immigration and Customs Enforcement (ICE) agent who pulled me over treated me like I was a damned dog. I've paid a lot of money in state and federal taxes, yet I get treated like that when I'm riding my motorcycle down a public highway.

THE EARLY CLUB SCENE

At the end of the nineteenth century, people formed clubs around just about anything. There were clubs devoted to collecting butterflies, examining dinosaur fossils, and studying electricity. When Gottlieb Daimler first bolted a gasoline engine to his two-wheeled *Einspur* and created the original motorcycle in 1885, it was inevitable that people would form clubs based around this new invention.

One of the earliest national motorcycle clubs in the United States, the Federation of American Motorcyclists (FAM), formed in 1903. It oversaw most officially sanctioned racing in the US. In 1924, after the FAM had folded, the Motorcycle Manufacturers Association (M&ATA), which represented the business end of motorcycling, formed the American Motorcycle Association (AMA) to represent the interests of riders.

The AMA became the official sanctioning body for motorcycle racing after the demise of the FAM, and it also oversaw most motorcycle clubs in the country. Because of its close association with the motorcycle manufacturers, the AMA was obsessed with

motorcycling's public image. It bombarded the public with propaganda designed to promote the image of the motorcyclist as a solid, socially responsible citizen, leading to cartoon characters like "Muffler Mike," who schooled motorcyclists on the evils of loud exhaust pipes. By the time the United States entered World War II, the AMA was sanctioning hundreds of motorcycle clubs and sponsoring over 750 events per year.

Motorcycle clubs remained popular throughout the first half of the twentieth century, but after World War II their popularity spiked. Most able-bodied American men had served in the military during the war, and many of them missed

the brotherhood they had shared with their fellow soldiers. Motorcycle clubs offered these veterans a way to recreate that camaraderie. By 1947, when the infamous bash in Hollister, California (see page 139), took place, there were dozens of clubs on the West Coast alone.

But not everyone was interested in wholesome AMA-sanctioned clubs engaged in family-oriented activities. This was especially true of the disaffected vets coming home from the horrors of war. They craved the excitement they had experienced during war, and putting on goofy club uniforms—complete with jodhpurs and silly little cop hats—and riding in tight-knit formations with a herd of other conformists held little appeal for such men.

These riders still wanted the camaraderie and brotherhood found in a club, so they formed clubs outside of the AMA—a move that didn't please the AMA one bit. The AMA referred to these unsanctioned clubs as "outlaws." Given that the members of these clubs thought the AMA was a ridiculous organization, they embraced the term, flaunting it as a metaphorical up-thrust middle finger aimed at the AMA oligarchy.

The motorcycle club scene changed dramatically after the Fourth of July weekend in 1947, when a motorcycle rally in the small town of Hollister, California, got a little boisterous. About 4,000 motorcycle riders came to town that weekend, mostly to attend races sponsored by the AMA. That was a quite a few more people than the town expected, and things got a little hectic.

Eyewitness reports tell of such things as motorcyclists throwing water balloons off balconies, popping wheelies on Main Street, and generally riding around whooping and hollering like drunken fools. There were a few fights, and more than a little street racing, but other than a couple tools being stolen from a tire repair shop and one guy was arrested for pissing in the radiator of a car that was overheating, there was no real crime to speak of.

A total of 29 people were arrested for drunkenness, indecent exposure, and traffic violations. Finally, one guy rode his motorcycle right into a bar, prompting the owner to call the California Highway Patrol. The state troopers showed up, cleared everyone out, and put a stop to the festivities.

The Hollister event would have gone down in history as just another drunken Fourth of July party in a small town, had not a photographer put a pile of empty beer bottles around a motorcycle and had a guy pose on the bike. He sold the resulting photo to *Life* magazine, which became part of a story that eventually led to the 1953 film *The Wild One*.

After the film's release, just riding a motorcycle practically became a crime. Cops would harass riders at every opportunity simply because of their chosen mode of transportation. Faced with this kind of pressure, it makes sense that riders would seek the brotherhood found in motorcycle clubs.

"WE HAD LONGER WAYS TO GO. BUT NO MATTER, THE ROAD IS LIFE."

—JACK KEROUAC

13 REBELS, BOOZEFIGHTERS, AND GALLOPING GEESE

A few of the early "outlaw" motorcycle clubs achieved legendary status. Established in 1937, the 13 Rebels Motorcycle Club typify the outlaw clubs that dotted the United States prior to World War II, though the term "outlaw" is a bit of a stretch, at least as the term is used today. By today's standards, they were more of what Sonny Barger calls "mom-and-pop clubs." It might be better to think of them as two-percenters than as one-percenters. For example, the 13 Rebels MC kicked out a member named "Wino Willie" Forkner for drinking too much.

Willie went on to found another early club, the Boozefighters, one of the clubs that had participated in the "Hollister riot." This club served as one of the primary inspirations for the Black Rebels Motorcycle Club, the fictional club to which Marlon Brando's character Johnny belonged in the film *The Wild One*.

Willie and a group of fellow World War II vets established the Boozefighters MC as a Los Angeles-based club in 1946. Now in its eighth decade of existence, the Boozefighters continue to be an active part of the motorcycle club scene.

The Galloping Goose MC is another motorcycle club that dates back to the earliest days of the motorcycle club movement. Formed in the early 1940s, the club took its unusual name from a motorcycle called the "Galloping Goose," owned by a fellow named Dick Hershberg. Hershberg and his friends hung out in a Los Angeles bar called the Pullman in the early 1940s, then formed the club after they returned from the war.

The Galloping Goose MC is remembered today primarily because, like the Boozefighters, the GGMC were major players at the original Hollister event in 1947. The GGMC are, like the Boozefighters, more of a two-percent club than a hardcore MC, but that doesn't keep them off the radar of law enforcement.

THE ONE-PERCENTERS

When most people think of motorcycle clubs, they think of "one-percenter" clubs. This phrase comes from an oft-repeated legend in which an AMA spokesperson claims that 99 percent of all motorcyclists belonged to AMA-sanctioned clubs, meaning they were good, responsible citizens. This mythical spokesperson allegedly attributed all the trouble covered in the media at the time to the "one percent" of motorcyclists who belonged to "outlaw" clubs, hoodlums and thugs who had the balls to form clubs not sanctioned by the AMA. Though there have been many sensational events perpetrated by what the AMA considers outlaw clubs, much of what has been reported is exaggerated or outright fabricated. Even the legendary AMA proclama-tion cited above may well be apocryphal, since no one has ever provided a print record of this or even cited a source other than the vague "AMA spokesperson."

Regardless, the one percent title stuck and has become a badge of honor among club members who consider one-percenter clubs elite organizations to which members devote their entire lives.

Most one-percenter club members wear some sort of garment that features the club's patch (often called "colors") centered on the back of the garment, where it can be seen while the man is riding his motorcycle. (As politically incorrect as this may be, no one-percenter clubs allow women to be members—clubs that allow women members are by nature not one-percenter clubs.) That garment is

> "AT ANY MOMENT I EXPECTED TO HEAR THAT THE ANGELS HAD DRIVEN THEIR MOTORCYCLES STRAIGHT INTO THE SEA, WHICH HAD ROLLED BACK TO LET THEM PASS."
>
> —HUNTER S. THOMPSON, *HELL'S ANGELS: A STRANGE AND TERRIBLE SAGA OF THE OUTLAW MOTORCYCLE GANGS*

traditionally sewn on a denim vest, or more accurately a denim jacket with the sleeves cut off (which is why it's often called a "cut"). Today, it's more common to see the patch sewn on a leather vest or jacket.

One-percenter patches usually consist of three parts: a central patch depicting the club's insignia, a rocker patch (a curved bar) on top with the club's name, and another rocker patch below indicating the particular charter of a club. This type of three-piece patch usually signifies that a club is a one-percenter club, but not always. Likewise, if a patch is a two-piece or one-piece patch, that usually (but not always) means the club is not a one-percenter club.

One-percenter clubs are as varied as the individuals who make up their memberships. Some clubs consist of single groups located in specific geographic areas; others are composed of charters spread around the country, or even the globe.

JOINING A ONE-PERCENTER CLUB

Membership in one-percenter clubs is usually gained through some variation of the following process: introduction, hang-around status, sponsorship, prospect phase, and, finally, either membership or failure. The would-be prospect first reaches the provisional status of a "hang-around." This is when club members have privately voted to make official the hang-around's status of club associate. If and when a club member deems the hang-around worthy of sponsorship as a prospect and is willing to act as the person's mentor, that member meets with the individual and offers to sponsor him. At a club meeting, the member stands up for the potential prospect and asks for a vote authorizing "prospect" status. By doing this, the member becomes responsible for the prospect. If a majority of members agree, the prospect is brought into the meeting, told of his new status, and given the bottom rocker "prospect" patch.

The official recognition as "prospect" marks the beginning of the prospect's hardcore testing phase, which may take many months, or even years. The prospect is given menial tasks, such as cleaning the clubhouse, helping set up for meetings and events, running errands, and maintaining members' bikes. Occasionally, he is also trusted with more significant jobs that require greater skill, creativity, or finesse; these assignments will come directly from the prospect's sponsor, upon whom the quality of the prospect's performance will reflect.

When the sponsoring member feels the time is right, he brings the prospect's membership to a vote before the whole club. This involves an open discussion among the members regarding the prospect's fitness as a potential club member. In most clubs, a unanimous vote is required to grant membership. When the vote is taken, if only one member votes against granting membership, that member must explain his reasons, in case he knows something the others do not.

If the members do not grant membership at this time, they decide whether to continue the prospect phase or dismiss the prospect entirely. If they do agree to make the prospect a member, they may invite the person into the meeting to congratulate him, or they may keep it a secret so they can surprise the prospect with his full patch at another time.

THE HELLS ANGELS

In 1957, seven men, one of whom was Sonny Barger, formed a motorcycle club in Oakland, California. They had found an old club patch that featured a flaming skull and the words "Hells Angels Motorcycle Club." They knew nothing about the history of the patch, but they liked the image and they liked the name, so they named their club "The Hells Angels MC."

When Barger and his buddies formed the Oakland-based Hells Angels MC, they had no idea that they were part of a larger existing organization. In *Let's Ride*, Barger describes learning about the existence of other charters of the Hells Angels:

> *In 1958 I rode with a guy named Ernie Brown, who was the vice president of the club I was in at the time. We'd ridden down to Los Angeles and my transmission blew up. We were sitting on the side of the road when another motorcyclist named Vic Bettencourt stopped to help. It turned out that he was the president of a charter of the same club.*

> *I didn't even know our club had a charter down there. We'd founded our club because we'd found a defunct club with a cool patch and we liked the patch. We didn't even know there were other charters of the club. It was the first time we realized we were part of something bigger than just the club my friends and I had started. Vic took us to their clubhouse and put a new transmission in my bike. He also taught me a lot about what brotherhood was all about.*

From that chance meeting between Barger and his new club brothers in Los Angeles, the Hells Angels MC has grown into one of the largest and most infamous motorcycle clubs on Earth, which charters around the globe.

"THE WISEST MEN FOLLOW THEIR OWN DIRECTION."

—EURIPIDES

THE BANDIDOS, PAGANS, OUTLAWS, AND SONS OF SILENCE

The Hells Angels aren't the only major motorcycle club with charters around the world. Together with the Bandidos, Pagans, Outlaws, and Sons of Silence, they comprise what author Bill Hayes calls "the big five" one-percenter clubs.

Ex-marine Don Chambers, a veteran of the Vietnam War, established the Bandidos MC in Texas on March 4, 1966. Chambers clearly brought some demons home when he returned from service in Southeast Asia; he was convicted of murder in Texas in 1972 and given a life sentence. Paroled in 1983, he did not return to the club and died on July 18, 1999.

The Bandidos MC became a worldwide organization. Although the Bandidos are considered a hardcore one-percenter motorcycle club, the venue in which they have the highest profile is in professional motorcycle drag racing. The Bandidos racing team is one of the most successful teams on the All Harley Drag Racing Association (AHDRA) drag-racing circuit.

> "NEITHER THE MOUSE NOR THE BOY WAS THE LEAST BIT SURPRISED THAT EACH COULD UNDERSTAND THE OTHER. TWO CREATURES WHO SHARED A LOVE FOR MOTORCYCLES NATURALLY SPOKE THE SAME LANGUAGE."
>
> —BEVERLY CLEARY, *THE MOUSE AND THE MOTORCYCLE*

Maryland-based Lou Dobkin founded the Pagans MC in 1959. The Pagans remained regional until around 1965, when the club began to expand around the Northeastern United States. The club's patch depicts the Norse fire-giant Surtr sitting on the sun, wielding a sword, an image based on an illustration by legendary comic book artist Jack Kirby.

Founded in 1935, the Outlaws MC is one of the oldest non-AMA-sanctioned motorcycle clubs in the world. Initially based in McCook, Illinois, a suburb southwest of Chicago, the club was originally called the McCook Outlaws. After World War II, the club relocated to Chicago. Like the Pagans, the club began to expand in the 1960s, forming the Florida charter of the Outlaws MC in 1965.

The club's original patch featured a winged motorcycle, but by 1954 this had been replaced by a pair of pistons forming pirate-like crossbones below a skull, which club members named "Charlie." Today, the Outlaws MC are as famous for their motto—"God forgives, Outlaws don't"—as they are for their logo. The club now includes charters around the world, and includes among its ex-members musician David Alan Coe.

The Sons of Silence originally formed in Colorado in 1966, but by 1968 they began forming charters in other states. In 1998, the club formed its first charter outside the United States in Munich, Germany, and today has charters around the world.

OTHER ONE-PERCENTER CLUBS

During World War II, a Mississippi sharecropper moved to Oakland, California, to get one of the tens of thousands of factory jobs created when the previous workers holding those jobs were sent to Europe and Japan. The sharecropper's son, Tobie Gene Levingston, happened to be a gearhead; when he was old enough to drive, he formed the East Bay Dragons. At first the Dragons were a car club, but Tobie oversaw the club's conversion to a motorcycle club. Eventually, the Dragons became one of the premiere African-American motorcycle clubs.

The Dragons found themselves at the epicenter of a number of major movements of the 1960s. They were part of the sex, drugs, and rock-and-roll scene that turned Haight-Ashbury into a hippie ghetto during the Summer of Love. The Dragons were friends with the Oakland charter of the Hells Angels MC, at the time headed by Sonny Barger, as well as the Black Panthers, hanging out with Black Panthers cofounders Huey Newton, Bobby Seale, and David Hilliard.

The BPM motorcycle club is a good example of a regional one-percenter club. What the name means is open to conjecture, but the best guess is that it stands for "booze, pussy, motorcycles." Located in the Upper Midwest, the BPMs are a genuine one-percenter club, definitely not people to be dismissed lightly, though those of us who came of age in the region have been riding and partying with BPMs all of our lives. If this author had been inclined to join a one-percenter club, the BPMs would have been the only logical choice—in fact, said author got his first tattoo from Magoo, an iconic member of the club.

Though those of us who grew up around the BPMs consider them just fellow motorcyclists, the same cannot be said for law-enforcement agencies. While members of the club undoubtedly engage in at least as much criminal activities as the rest of us, this author can personally attest to having committed far more crimes than he has ever witnessed being committed by members of the club, with whom he has spent a great deal of time.

To be fair, at least one member of the BPMs has been convicted, though he was wearing another club's patch at the time. In the early 1990s, the Minneapolis charter of the BPMs patched over

to the Hells Angels. In 2003, Pat Matter, president of the Minneapolis charter of the HAMC, pleaded guilty to money laundering and conspiracy to distribute cocaine and methamphetamine. Matter provided evidence against other members of the club, but, because of misconduct by the IRS, all the convictions garnered from his testimony were dismissed.

Although never a major player in the one-percenter club scene, the Coffin Cheaters MC, established in Long Beach, California, in the early 1960s have one claim to fame: members of the original CCMC appeared beside members of the Hells Angels MC in the 1966 film *The Wild Angels*.

While the Long Beach–based Coffin Cheaters MC never branched out, the club name itself did become international. In the early 1970s, a group of motorcyclists formed the Australian Coffin Cheaters MC. Whether the name was inspired by the credits from *The Wild Angels* is open to conjecture, but given the worldwide success of Roger Corman and Peter Fonda's biker flick, it seems unlikely that the Australian founders of the Coffin Cheaters MC weren't aware of the club name. Regardless of the name's origin, the club has thrived down under, with three charters in Perth, two in Victoria, two in New South Wales, and two in Queensland. There are also three CCMC charters in Norway.

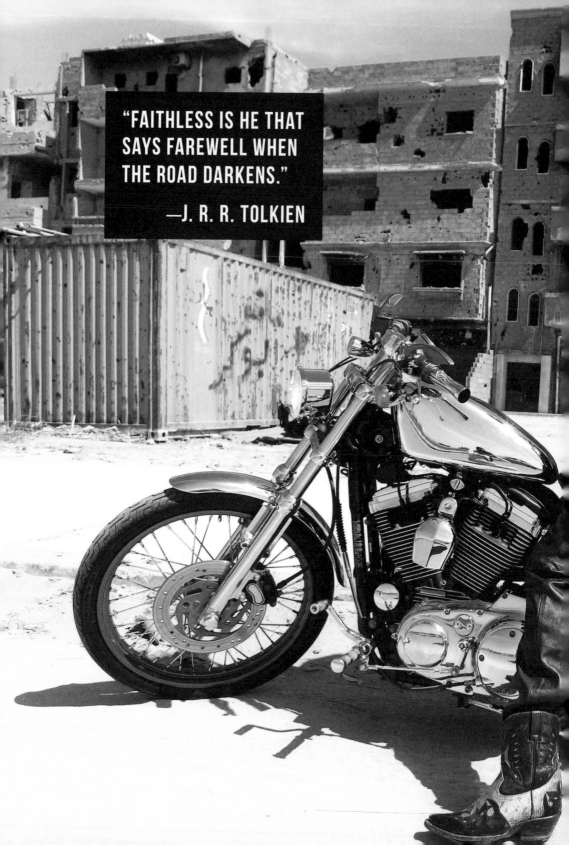

"FAITHLESS IS HE THAT SAYS FAREWELL WHEN THE ROAD DARKENS."

—J. R. R. TOLKIEN

FULL CIRCLE

Today we're seeing the rise of a new breed of motorcycle club, one that doesn't have a giant log up its collective ass—as did the old uniformed AMA clubs—but one that also doesn't embrace the traditional outlaw esthetic and all the legal baggage that comes with it. These clubs hearken back to the early days of clubs like the Boozefighters and the Galloping Goose MC, collections of fun-loving riders, people who like to blow off a little steam. Think of them as beer drinkers and cannabis enthusiasts with motorcycle problems.

One example of this new breed is the Douche LaRouche MC, a group of imaginative young people who love to have a good time and who also happen to love classic customized motorcycles. Perhaps the best way to understand the Douche LaRouche MC is to let them explain the club in their own words, as taken from the "Who are we?" section of the club's website:

I am writing today from a bunker in an undisclosed location in an effort to dissuade you from digging any deeper into the Douche LaRouche Motorcycle Club (DLMC) organization

. . . . What I can tell you for sure is that there is a definite connection between this group of lovable moto-jesters and a source of evil so overwhelmingly frightening that I almost cannot bring myself to type these words. Think inter-dimensional scary-ass monster demons from mythological times. Although I personally have not been able to concretely establish what the connection is, several independent researchers (all who have mysteriously passed away) speculated off the record that a lineage could very well exist between current DLMC members and a group of ancient warriors responsible for keeping peace and order between our world and the realm of the shadow dwellers . . . .

While it's safe to assume there's a certain amount of hyperbole in this description, it does capture the nature of this new breed of club—riders who love motorcycles and love having fun, but who don't take themselves as seriously as clubs of yore. The club scene, it seems, has come full circle.

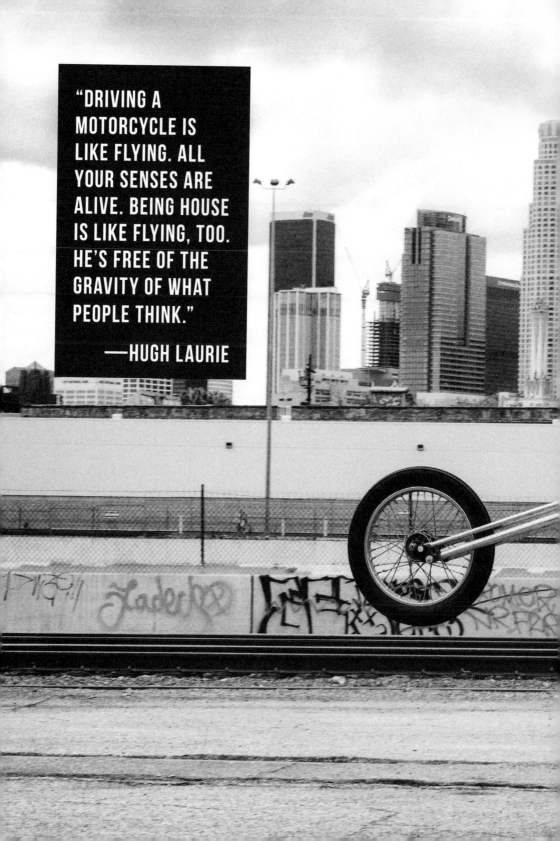

"DRIVING A MOTORCYCLE IS LIKE FLYING. ALL YOUR SENSES ARE ALIVE. BEING HOUSE IS LIKE FLYING, TOO. HE'S FREE OF THE GRAVITY OF WHAT PEOPLE THINK."

—HUGH LAURIE

CHAPTER FOUR

THE POP CULTURE LIFE

FROM THE WILD ONE TO AN EASY RIDER

Which came first: the biker or the biker film? It might seem a ridiculous question, but it has more merit than one might imagine.

The public's concept of the biker and the biker-film genre both began at the same time and in the same place: Hollister, California, at the 1947 Gypsy Tour. Gypsy Tours were organized rides, often multiday affairs, organized around other motorcycle-related activities like racing or hill climbing. These were usually held at the same time each year, and an especially popular Gypsy Tour was held in Hollister every Fourth of July.

As we saw in the previous chapter, Hollister proved a pivotal event in the life Harley-Davidson. The 1947 "riot" would have been a non event, had it not been for photographer Barney Peterson taking what appear to have been staged photos that sensationalized the event. These photos ran in the July 7 issue of the *San Francisco Chronicle* and appeared in *Life* magazine a week later.

Today, these photos would seem relatively harmless, but the world was a very different place in 1947. People lived in fear of, well, pretty much everything. These were the early years of the Cold War, and many Americans were terrified. Using the excuse of Communist infiltrators, the US government began a Draconian crackdown on intellectuals, labor unions, immigrants, people of color, young people in general, and pretty much anyone else who didn't conform to a rigid code of behavior. People were as afraid of being labeled *communistas* they were of Communists themselves, and people strove to look and behave in as homogeneous a fashion as possible.

Most people, anyway. Motorcyclists, not so much. Hollister had just been another rowdy weekend for them, but to the Leave-It-to-Beaverized average citizen, these two-wheeled miscreants represented what Hunter S. Thompson

called "the menace," filthy subhuman animals whose behavior was too horrible to contemplate.

The Hollister event captured the public's imagination and didn't let go. Eventually the horrific imagery that Peterson captured on film made its way into popular culture. The January 1951 issue of *Harper's* magazine featured a short story by author Frank Rooney inspired by Hollister. "Cyclists' Raid" told of a motorcycle gang taking over a town. Rooney wrote: "Now there were other motorcycles on the sidewalk. One of them hit a parked car at the edge of the walk. The rider standing astride his machine beat the window out of the car with his gloved fists." Terrifying stuff, that.

In 1953, producer Stanley Kramer released *The Wild One*, a celluloid version of Rooney's short story, and the world was changed forever.

COMMIES AND BIKERS

To fully understand the impact of *The Wild One* requires a bit of background information. Most importantly, one needs to understand that it's not really a biker film—it's a Marlon Brando film. More specifically, it's a Stanley Kramer–produced Marlon Brando film. That last bit is important because of the situation in which Kramer found himself at the time of production.

Befitting the producer of a film about a rebel, Kramer had earned his reputation by rebelling against the studio culture that controlled Hollywood in the 1930s and '40s. Because he didn't conform to that rigid culture, he had difficulty finding work, so he formed his own production company, Screen Plays Inc. In addition to being a talented writer and producer, Kramer proved a clever business person and devised ways to produce films for a fraction of the cost of films produced by the major studios. This helped the studio thrive amid the glut of independent production companies that sprang up during the period. What really differentiated Screen Plays Inc. (later renamed Stanley Kramer Company) was its fearlessness in tackling taboo subjects like social justice and making political statements with its films.

Kramer struck gold with a string of successful films like *Champion*, which marked the acting debut of an ex-wrestler named Kirk Douglas, *Home of the Brave*, which tackled the subject of anti-Semitism, and *The Men*, featuring Marlon Brando in his first screen role as a paraplegic war veteran. This brought Kramer to the attention of Harry Cohen, who brought Stanley Kramer Company under the corporate umbrella of Columbia Pictures.

On the surface, things seemed to be going swimmingly, but that wasn't really the case. Two factors had thrown Hollywood into complete chaos: television and Wisconsin Senator Joseph McCarthy. The new technology of television was cannibalizing customers from theater seats, and McCarthy's witch hunt against suspected Hollywood Communists was draining talent, wrecking personal relationships, and destroying lives.

McCarthy's Senate hearings grew out of the infamous House Un-American Activities Committee (HUAC) investigations into the alleged disloyalty and subversive activities on the part of private citizens, public employees, and those organizations suspected of having Communist ties. HUAC's real purpose was

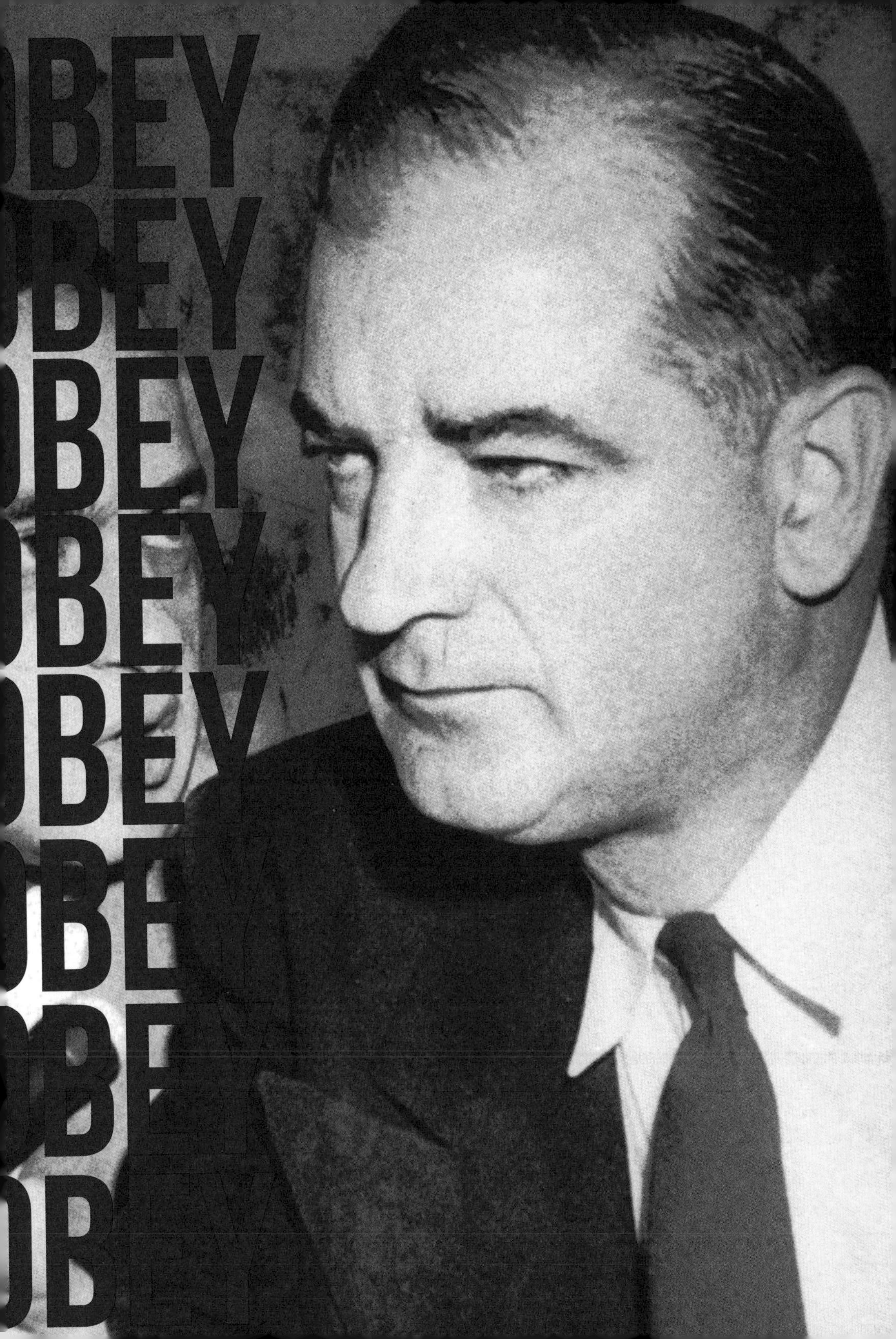

to roll back the gains labor had made under the progressive policies of Franklin Roosevelt's New Deal; being able to terrify people into submission and obedience was just gravy. HUAC's main tactic was to pressure witnesses into surrendering names and other information that could lead to the apprehension of Communists and Communist sympathizers. HUAC branded witnesses as being "reds" or "fellow travelers" if they refused to comply or hesitated in answering committee questions, which led to their being blacklisted—being added to secret lists that made them unemployable.

McCarthy used these techniques in his Senate hearings, which focused on high-profile academics and celebrities for maximum impact. In April 1951, McCarthy's committee summoned Carl Foreman, who had received an Academy Award nomination for his screenplay for Champion. Foreman refused to testify and was branded a Red. Kramer, who at the time was coproducing Foreman's screenplay of *High Noon* with Fred Zinnemann, initially fired Foreman as the screenwriter; pressure from Zinnemann and the film's star Gary Cooper forced Kramer to reinstate Foreman.

A pissed-off Kramer engaged in a public campaign against Foreman, thus aligning himself with other right-wing figures in Hollywood like John Wayne, Hedda Hopper, and Ronald Reagan, and with reactionary organizations like the Motion Picture Alliance for the Preservation of American Ideals (MPAPAI). This estranged Kramer from the more progressive figures in Hollywood. Ever the rebel, Kramer defied Hollywood's liberal contingent by making a series of films that demonized elements he considered subversive, such as unions, the working class, young people in general—and, in one particular instance, young people who rode motorcycles.

The antihero biker archetype existed before *The Wild One* was released, but it existed on a very small scale. In the early 1950s, the total number of people in what would become known as "outlaw motorcycle clubs" would not have filled a high school auditorium.

THE ALPHA DOG: THE WILD ONE

That all changed in 1953. *The Wild One* turned what was a small-scale counterculture based primarily on the West Coast into a worldwide phenomenon. It also spawned an entire film genre, one that supplanted the Western as the quintessential American film genre in the latter half of the twentieth century. For those who haven't seen *The Wild One*, it's not a biker film in the traditional sense; it's first and foremost a Marlon Brando film. Like all Brando films, it's loaded with subtle homoerotic imagery. For example, compare the dance scene in *The Wild One* to the dance scene in Al Pacino's 1980 film *Cruising*, which explores the seedy underbelly of gay clubs, and you'll see remarkable similarities. Brando, who was famously fluid about his sexuality, included homoerotic elements in his films throughout his career.

Like Mel Gibson, Brando also seemed to have some sort of messiah complex; virtually every film in which he starred featured some sort of crucifixion scene. Again, *The Wild One* was no exception— toward the end of the film, Brando is nearly beaten to death by the angry townsfolk, saved only by the intervention of The Man in the form of local Sheriff Harry Bleeker.

> "THE FILM MIGHT HAVE SCARED THE SHIT OUT OF AVERAGE AMERICANS, BUT WHEN MY FRIENDS AND I SAW THE WILD ONE AS TEENAGERS, WE WANTED TO BE JUST LIKE CHINO."
>
> —SONNY BARGER. HELLS ANGEL

This is also a post-McCarthy Stanley Kramer film. Having gotten pushback from Hollywood's liberal contingent after trying to fire writer Carl Foreman from *High Noon*, Kramer was a man with a mission, and that mission was to exonerate himself and anti-Communist reactionary ideology in general. Thus *The Wild One* was a message film, and the message was that insidious and terrifying outside forces were going to take over our towns, molest our womenfolk, destroy our private property, and generally sodomize our American way of life. Judging by the furor that the film unleashed, Kramer succeeded. *The Wild One* was considered so shocking that it was banned in England. In the States, the Motion Picture Production Code—commonly known as the Hays Code—the body that set and enforced the moral guidelines for what was and was not acceptable in movies—would only approve *The Wild One* if Marlon Brando read what amounted to a disclaimer in a voiceover at the beginning of the film. Compelled but not defeated, Brando surrendered under protest; he read the disclaimer but mumbled his lines, rendering his monologue virtually unintelligible.

To some degree, Brando's Johnny character informed the cultural stereotype of the biker. The vaguely homoerotic sexual ambiguity of Johnny is reflected in the historic figure of the leather-clad biker, although the Johnny character is more prominently represented in the gay community itself. Even the one-percenter motorcycle club culture has hints of this homoeroticism,

although one-percenters tongue-kissing one another in public is usually done more for shock value than as an expression of man-on-man lust.

The character who really set the mold for the stereotypical biker was Chino, played by Lee Marvin. Appearing on screen for less than ten minutes as the leader of a rival motorcycle club called The Beetles, those ten minutes forever shaped the world's a priori concept of "biker." Marvin's rough, crude, violent, and oddly charming Chino defined what it would mean to be a biker.

Chino had balls, and he knew how to have fun. He wasn't out looking to push anyone around; he just wanted to ride his motorcycle and have a good time.

Though the film seems dated and corny by modern standards, it was generally well-reviewed at the time, and no one can deny that Brando and Marvin turned in stellar performances, cementing Brando's reputation as one of the twentieth century's greatest sex symbols and elevating Marvin's Chino to the status of proto-urbiker, the biker archetype that all future bikers would try to emulate.

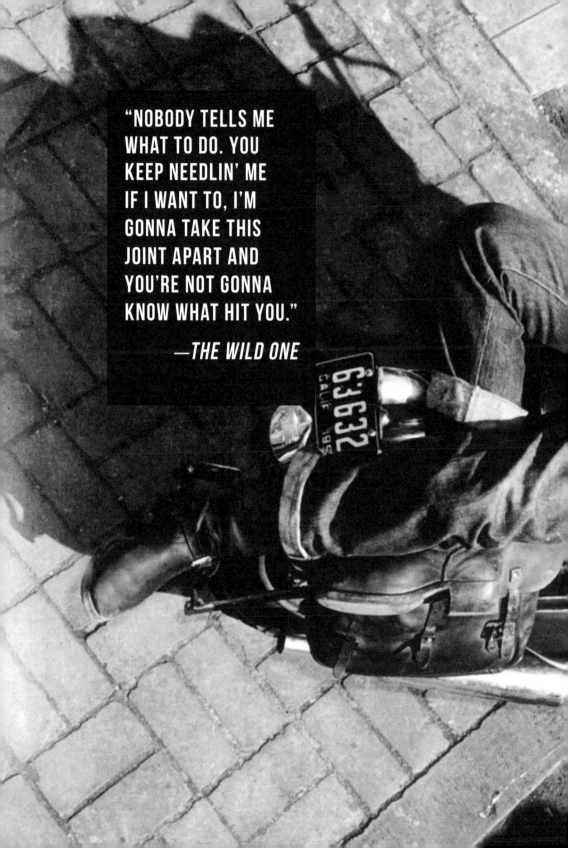

"NOBODY TELLS ME
WHAT TO DO. YOU
KEEP NEEDLIN' ME
IF I WANT TO, I'M
GONNA TAKE THIS
JOINT APART AND
YOU'RE NOT GONNA
KNOW WHAT HIT YOU."

—*THE WILD ONE*

THROBBING PISTONS AND GIANT JUGS

Given the commercial success of *The Wild One*, it was inevitable that other biker flicks would follow, films like 1957's *Motorcycle Gang* and 1958's *Hot Angel*.

In *Motorcycle Gang*, which set the mold for the genre, a motorcycle club rides roughshod through rural America, which, apparently, was pretty much all that motorcycle clubs did. The club might have been riding roughshod, but not roughshod enough for Nick, who, upon returning from a 15-month stint in the pokey, thinks the club has gone soft. They're hanging out at a café managed by The Man (local sheriff Watson), collecting membership dues, and enforcing rules like banning members who've had parking tickets from competing in races. Nick thinks this is pure bullshit and spends most of his time trying to bang club moll Terry.

Terry is fascinated by Nick, but she's not quite free enough to go all the way with this bad boy fresh out of prison. Somehow all of this culminates into Nick and his main rival racing their motorcycles across a railroad bridge, which, as one might expect, goes horribly wrong. Nick's rival goes to the hospital. Nick spins even more out of

control and tries to rape Terry. After that sordid incident, Nick and some of his thug buddies get drunk and hold some people hostage in a restaurant for reasons that are never made clear. Somehow the producers manage to squeeze in another motorcycle race before Nick is finally arrested, saving the good townspeople from further motorcycle mayhem.

This set the general template for "biker gang" films for the next decade, with each new installment in the franchise trying to one-up the last in portrayals of shocking outlaw behavior. To judge by these films, riding a motorcycle transformed a formerly civilized young man into a raping, rampaging beast. In each film, the rampages became a little rampagier and the (usually attempted) rapes became a little rapier. The violence became a little more violent, and the tattered clothing of the rape victim showed a little more flesh, creeping ever closer to the sacrosanct nipple. It was only a matter of time before boob fetishist Russ Meyer got in on this action.

Meyer earned his reputation peddling soft porn—what has come to be known as "breastploitation"—

ON THE
[I]NES!

[...]ding
[...]UMS
[...]UT on
[...]URDER

AN EVE PRODUCTION
Produced and Directed by RUSS MEYER

Motor Psycho

Starring STEPHEN OLIVER, with HAJI, ALEX ROCCO, HOLLE K. WINTERS, JOSEPH CELLINI, SHARON LEE and THOMAS SCO[...]

...in the
[DE]ADLIEST
[CYC]LE WAR
ever
waged!

DENNIS HOPPER · JODY McCREA · CHRIS NOEL · JOCK MA[...]
STARRING IN
THE GLORY STOMPE[RS]

with titles like *Wild Gals of the Naked West*, *Mondo Topless*, and *Skyscrapers & Brassieres*. Despite having no actual nudity, his 1965 *Motorpsycho* brought a new level of raciness to the biker flick genre. Led by psycho Vietnam War vet Brahman, the "bikers" ride mopeds instead of chopped Harleys, but they engage in a level of mayhem that would have made *Motorcycle Gang*'s bad boy Nick blush. What the film's antagonists lack in cubic displacement, they more than make up for in rapiness and violence. After the moped-mounted miscreants rape veterinarian Cory's wife, all hell breaks loose. Cory follows them to the desert, where he meets the widow of a man the moped-riding marauders have just murdered, and the two team up to rampage against the villains, resulting in an orgy of violence and breasts.

Though it had a certain bizarre charm, like all of Meyer's films, *Motorpsycho* was bad enough that it might have killed the biker-flick genre for good, but for the intervention of a second-generation Hollywood star (and card-carrying biker) with aspirations toward being the American version of French filmmaker Jean Rouch, inventor of *cinema vérité*.

AND WE WANT TO GET LOADED!

Born February 23, 1940, to Hollywood actor Henry Fonda and New York socialite Frances Seymour Brokaw, Peter Fonda grew up in the shadow of his famous father. Fonda excelled in school and enrolled in the University of Omaha as a sophomore at 17, before he'd even finished high school. Fonda first took up the family business of acting in Omaha, where he appeared in the Omaha Playhouse's production of *Harvey*. He moved to New York to pursue acting; in 1961, at the age of 21, he made his Broadway debut in a production of *Blood, Sweat and Stanley Poole*. In 1963, he made his film debut in the Sandra Dee film *Tammy and the Doctor*.

Fonda approached filmmaking with the same scholarly bent that had helped make him a 17-year-old college sophomore. He was heavily influenced by French filmmaker Jean Rouch's cinema vérité style, in which actors improvised dialogue and the director used the camera to capture the truths hidden behind crude reality. In his book *Easy Riders and Raging Bulls*, author Peter Biskind quotes Fonda describing his filmmaking style as "cinema vérité in allegory terms."

The intellectual Fonda found his foil in the form of B-movie producer Roger Corman. The Detroit-born Corman, fourteen years Fonda's senior, earned a degree in engineering from Stanford but worked just three days as an engineer before quitting to pursue his real passion: film. After working his way up the food chain at 20th Century Fox, eventually becoming a story analyst, he left to study English at Oxford University, hoping to become a screenwriter and producer. He sold his first script in 1953 and eventually ended up working at what would become American-International Pictures, where he wrote, produced, and directed films at a fast and furious pace.

In 1960, he cranked out *Little Shop of Horrors* in just two-and-one-half days. He earned critical acclaim for a series of Vincent Price films based on Edgar Allan Poe stories and then attempted his most serious project to date: 1962's *The Intruder*, starring William Shatner. While the film won critical praise— and a prize at the Venice Film Festival—it was a commercial failure. Corman decided he'd rather produce exploitation movies that made money than critically acclaimed films that lost money.

In 1966, it seemed that the genre of the biker flick might be running out of steam, but Corman and Fonda were about to give it a new lease on life. At the request of Sam Arkoff and Jack Nicholson, Corman agreed to produce a film called *The Wild Angels*. Charles Griffith penned the original screenplay, though it was rewritten during the three weeks it took to film the project by a young Peter Bogdanovich. This would mark the first collaboration between Corman and Fonda.

Shot entirely on location in San Bernardino, the plot of *The Wild Angels*, revolves around the Wild Angels Motorcycle Club trying to help club member Loser, played by Bruce Dern, recover his stolen motorcycle from a chop shop in Mecca. Fonda plays Heavenly Blues, the president of the club, and members of the actual Hells Angels and Coffin Cheaters motorcycle clubs serve as extras. The inclusion of real bikers riding real motorcycles gave the film a fairly realistic atmosphere. The Loser lives up to his name and is shot by a police officer, so Blues and the rest of the club members get the bright idea of springing Loser from the hospital where he is being treated. The lack of foresight in this scheme becomes apparent when The Loser dies while smoking a joint on a Nazi flag-draped.

Though many members of motorcycle clubs were military veterans, motorcycle club culture made liberal use of Nazi symbolism in the 1960s. This was in part for shock value but it also meshed with the politics of many club members, who were nationalistic, totalitarian, and extremely racist. The irony of The Loser dying on a Nazi flag cannot be lost on anyone who has studied Nazi history. Hitler would have sent undisciplined non-conformists like The Loser straight to the camps. Be that as it may, The Loser does expire atop a giant swastika, leaving Blues and the club no choice but to have a funeral. They ride up into the mountains, take over a church, tie up the priest, and throw him into a coffin with The Loser's remains, then proceed to hold a drunken orgy. Since no biker flick worth its salt would have been rape-free in 1966, Dear John and Frankenstein rape The Loser's widow in the church. People tend to gloss over that bit of cinematic creepiness, but no one forgets Heavenly Blues' immortal soliloquy. When the priest asks Blues what the bikers want, Blues responds: "We wanna be free to ride our machines without being hassled by the man! And we wanna get loaded! And have a good time!"

Filmed for a budget of just $350,000, *The Wild Angels* went on to become one of the top-grossing films of 1966. *The Wild Angels'* unlikely success was that it allowed Fonda to produce and star in the cinema vérité biker flick he really wanted to make.

A STRANGE AND TERRIBLE SAGA

An astute reader may have noticed that the biker film genre seemed obsessed with rape. That was how Hollywood rolled. Demonizing a perceived enemy for having uncontrollable sexual appetites had a long tradition in American cinema.

In the years following the abolition of slavery, the propaganda against freed slaves portrayed them as out-of-control sexual predators, slaves to their basest desires. This terrified the white male population, which feared nothing more than their most prized possessions—their womenfolk—being violated.

This was the prevalent mindset in 1915, when D.W. Griffith filmed *The Birth of a Nation*, the first blockbuster film to come from Hollywood. The plot driver in the film, which is pure racist propaganda (and was also the first film ever screened in the White House), is the attempted rape of Flora Cameron by an ex-slave named Gus. Since Flora would lose all value as a symbol of pure white womanhood should she be sullied by Gus's dusky semen, she has no choice but to leap to her death. The noble Ku Klux Klan steps in and rescues another white woman (played by Lillian Gish) from a sex-crazed black militia.

Sound familiar? Substitute "filthy bikers" for "black militia" and you have the plot of every biker flick made between the release of *The Wild One* and *Easy Rider*. Although America had (and still has) a long way to go in ensuring equal rights for all its citizens, by the middle of the twentieth century America had at least progressed to a point where it was no longer socially acceptable to blatantly demonize Americans of African descent in film. (Racism in mainstream film continues to this day, but now it's a bit more subtle, hidden in subtexts.) Still Hollywood needed some alien Other with which to terrify the citizenry into submission. Commies were sort of scary, but a bunch of tweedy intellectuals with wire-rimmed glasses preaching socialism weren't nearly as sexy as dark-skinned villains. Or bikers. When it became socially unacceptable to overtly demonize people of because of their level of skin pigmentation, bikers provided a perfect substitution.

By the middle of the twentieth century, Stanley Kramer's motorcycle gangs had displaced D.W. Griffith's

black militias as the terrifying Other that was coming to rape white womanhood. And, to some degree, bikers were living up to their celluloid image.

On Labor Day weekend, 1964, Californians opened their newspapers to discover lascivious accounts of a gang rape that occurred at a Hells Angels party on the Monterey Peninsula. According to the reports, two girls, aged 14 and 15, were kidnapped and repeatedly raped by members of the Hells Angels Motorcycle Club. About 300 Hells Angels were at the gathering. Ultimately no charges were pressed. According to a report on motorcycle gangs compiled by the office of California Attorney General Thomas Lynch in 1965—the infamous "Lynch Report"—the Monterey case was dropped because "further investigation raised questions as to whether forcible rape had been committed or if the identifications made by victims were valid." The witnesses' testimonies contradicted one another, and at least one witness failed a lie detector test.

In *The Motorcycle Gangs*, published in the May 17, 1965, issue of *The Nation*, author Hunter S Thompson quotes a member of the Hells Angels who was present at the event:

One girl was white and pregnant, the other was colored, and they were with five colored studs. They hung around our bar—Nick's Place on Del Monte Avenue—for about three hours Saturday night, drinking and talking with our riders, then they came out to the beach with us— them and their five boyfriends. Everybody was standing around the fire, drinking wine, and some of the guys were talking to them—hustling 'em, naturally—and soon somebody asked the two chicks if they wanted to be turned on—you know, did they want to smoke some pot? They said yeah, and then they walked off with some of the guys to the dunes. The spade went with a few guys and then she wanted to quit, but the pregnant one was really hot to trot; the first four or five guys she was really dragging into her arms, but after that she cooled off, too. By this time, though, one of their boyfriends had got scared and gone for the cops— and that's all it was.

Yes. That was all it was. This event, the coverage it got in the mainstream press, and Thompson's coverage of it in *The Nation*—and later in his book *Hell's Angels: The Strange and Terrible Saga of the Outlaw Motorcycle Gangs*—speaks volumes about the motorcycle club culture of the era, of the public's perception of those clubs, and about societal mores in general during that period.

First off, this event was indeed rape. The fact that the girls wanted to stop having sex means that from that point on all sexual encounters constituted rape. It doesn't matter if one girl wanted to stop having sex after being with three partners and the other didn't want to stop until she'd been with more members of the club; the moment the girls said no, the event became rape. Even today, this would be a difficult case to prosecute, but few civilized people would argue that it wasn't rape.

At the time, the fact that the girls were sexually active devalued them as symbols of American womanhood, lessening their value in the propaganda war to demonize biker culture. Worse yet, one of the victims wasn't even white, and as the casual acceptance of racism in Thompson's *Nation* article shows, being white mattered even more in 1964 than it does today. To strike fear into the hearts of middle America—and at the time the only middle Americans that counted were as white as the Pillsbury Doughboy—the demonized Other had to rape women who symbolized purity and whiteness; pregnant women, who were obviously not pure, and women of color hardly counted.

The line had been drawn, the curse had been cast, and the image of the biker as a filthy beast that would maul, murder, and rape anyone it got its claws on had been set in stone. The success of Thompson's bestselling book and of Corman and Fonda's *The Wild Angels* meant that drive-ins across the country would be screening an endless loop of celluloid bikers raping and rampaging for the foreseeable future, films like *The Born Losers, The Glory Stompers, Hells Angels on Wheels, The Rebel Rousers, Wild Rebels, She-Devils on Wheels, The Cycle Savages, Hell's Belles, Hell's Angels '69, Naked Angels, Run, Angel, Run, and Angel Unchained.*

All biker flicks would follow the franchise formula of mindless raping and rampaging until Peter Fonda made *Easy Rider.*

> "SOME MAY NEVER LIVE, BUT THE CRAZY NEVER DIE."
>
> —HUNTER S. THOMPSON"

COMPLETING THE HOLY TRINITY

While there have been hundreds of biker flicks made since the release of *The Wild One*, three films comprise the holy trinity of the genre: *The Wild One*, *The Wild Angels*, and 1969's *Easy Rider*. Of the three, *Easy Rider* was the most significant.

First, it was by far the best film. *The Wild One* featured outstanding performances by Brando and Marvin, but as a film it falls a bit flat. The townsfolk are two-dimensional, all the bikers except Lee Marvin's Chino bear no resemblance whatsoever to most real humans who rode motorcycles

at the time, and the plot wasn't so much a plot as it was a piece of Stanley Kramer redbaiting apologia. Its success was more due to the fact that it exploited a new phenomenon that had captured the public's attention, it had exciting (for the period) action, and it featured Hollywood's hottest man alive: Marlon Brando.

The Wild Angels was pure exploitation and nothing more. Although it featured actors who would go on to earn critical acclaim, no critic ever acclaimed their performances in *The Wild Angels*. Nor did anyone praise any other aspect of the film. Most people have seen clips of Peter Fonda's immortal soliloquy quoted above, but few people watch the film today, because it's, well, awful. The racist Nazi symbolism horrifies modern viewers, women are objectified in ways that make bukkake porn seem like militant feminism, the plot is idiotic, the directing seems to be done by the accounting team, and the acting is terrible. Fonda was a motorcyclist and actual members of outlaw motorcycle clubs acted as extras, so the film does have a gritty realism, but that is the extent of its redeeming qualities.

> ## "'EASY RIDER' WAS NEVER A MOTORCYCLE MOVIE TO ME. A LOT OF IT WAS ABOUT POLITICALLY WHAT WAS GOING ON IN THE COUNTRY."
> —DENNIS HOPPER

Easy Rider was a whole different kettle of fish.

First, it was a genuinely good film, one with moments of greatness. Of all the 1960s biker flicks, it's by far the most watchable today. Fonda and costar Dennis Hopper turn in solid performances, and Hopper's direction is spot-on. The plot itself seems a bit clichéd today, the hippy-dippy idealism dated, and the symbolism so heavy-handed that at times it becomes cringeworthy. The most egregious example of Fonda and Hopper clubbing the viewer over the head with symbolism comes when we see their characters, Wyatt and Billy, repairing a tire on Fonda's chopper on a New Mexico ranch while the ranch owner shoes a horse in the background. Yes, we get it— Fonda and Hopper are modern-day cowboys, on steel horses they ride. Someone should write a song about that . . . .

Like the visual imagery, the dialog sounds dated and preachy at times, especially some of Fonda's lines. Fonda's Wyatt represents American idealism, youthful hope for the future, and generally that works surprisingly well in the film, but at times the filmmakers take it a step and a half too far. For example, when Wyatt tells the above-mentioned rancher, "It's not every man that can live off the land, you know. You do your own thing in your own time. You should be proud." Clearly the rancher knew this; he did not need some pretty boy from Los Angeles bestowing worthiness upon him.

Where Fonda's Wyatt represents American idealism, Hopper's Billy represents the ugly side of the American character. Billy is much more cynical, greedy, and lustful, and Hopper portrays those characteristics perfectly throughout the film. Hopper would go on to become one of the finest character actors of the latter half of the twentieth century, and his talent is evident even at this early stage in his career.

A few glitches aside, the film is the best of the early biker films by a long shot, and displays genuine moments of greatness, especially when Jack Nicholson is on screen. Fonda and Hopper mostly straddle the line between art and allegory

pretty well, but Nicholson's portrayal of small-town lawyer George Hanson is brilliant. From the instant Nicholson appears on screen, waking up in a drunk tank of a jail where Wyatt and Billy are locked up for parading without a permit, the film rises to a level not previously seen in a biker flick. Hanson assures the pair that he can get them out of jail, "if you haven't killed anybody . . . at least nobody white."

The unsung stars of the film are the motorcycles themselves. Designed and built by Benjamin "Ben" Hardy and Clifford Vaughs, a pair of African-American motorcycle customizers from South Central Los Angeles, Fonda's star-spangled chopper, nicknamed "Captain America," is an example of the wretched excess that characterized customs of the period, and Hopper's more traditional custom (nicknamed the "Billy Bike") is typical of the style of bike that black riders in the Los Angeles were building at the time. These bikes dominate the screen as much as Fonda, Hopper, and Nicholson themselves. Even though Wyatt and Billy come to bad ends at the hands of Louisiana duck hunters, the image of the pair out looking for America aboard those amazing custom Harleys was so potent that it inspired a generation of riders to head out on their own quests, shotgun-wielding rednecks be damned.

man went looking for America.
nd couldn't find it anywhere...

Cannes Film
Festival
WINNER
"Best Film
By a New
Director"

DO COMPANY in association with
ERT PRODUCTIONS presents **easy rider**

ng
ETER FONDA · DENNIS HOPPER · JACK NICHOL

en by   Directed by   Produced by   Associate Producer   Executive Producer
R FONDA   DENNIS HOPPER   PETER FONDA   WILLIAM HAYWARD   BERT SCHNEIDER · COL
IS HOPPER

Easy Rider changed everything. The third-highest-grossing film of 1969, behind *Bonnie and Clyde* and *The Graduate*, *Easy Rider* changed the way Hollywood films were made. Hollywood had been struggling, unable to reach the exploding baby boomer market with its traditional studio fare. Filmed for just $400,000, *Easy Rider* grossed $60 million worldwide, and nearly $42 million in the US alone. Most of that money came from the coveted youth market that had been ignoring Hollywood films in droves. The wild success of *Easy Rider* convinced film studios to fund a new wave of young, experimental filmmakers like Martin Scorsese and Francis Ford Coppola, ushering in a golden age of American film.

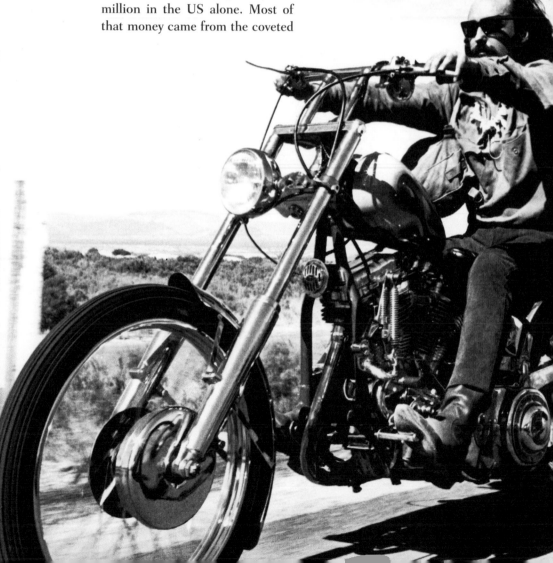

Easy Rider also changed the way that bikers were portrayed on screen. It was the first film since *The Wild One* a generation earlier not to depict at least one attempted rape. Hopper's ugly American Billy character behaves ugly and American, and Fonda's sensitive hippy poet biker Wyatt character behaves like a sensitive hippy poet biker. In the grand scheme of things, both characters behave in a much more civilized fashion than any previous character in a biker flick.Overnight, the celluloid biker went from two-dimensional cartoon villain to sympathetic antihero. Thus began the rehabilitation of the biker character in popular culture and of the actual biker in the greater world as well.

THEN CAME A NEW BIKER ARCHETYPE

Easy Rider presented a new type of cinematic biker: the thoughtful hippy poet whose only commonality with the raping and pillaging brutes shown in traditional biker flicks was the Harley-Davidson motorcycle between his legs. This sensitive intellectual biker would become increasingly common on the big screen.

On television, the image of the biker as an out-of-control, hormone-crazed beast would remain the norm. Television bikers continued raping and pillaging on the sets of such disparate television series as *Run for Your Life* and *The Rockford Files*, but the dreamy biker archetype created by Peter Fonda began to make inroads on the small screen, too. The most notable early example was James "Jim" Bronson, played by Michael Parks in the series *Then Came Bronson*, which aired on NBC in 1969–70.

Parks's Bronson, a reporter for the *San Francisco Chronicle*, becomes disillusioned after the suicide of his best friend Nick (played by Martin Sheen). Bronson gets into an argument with his editor, quits his job, and hits the open road aboard his motorcycle. The part of Bronson's motorcycle is played by

a 1969 XLH Sportster, which often has as much a starring role in the series as the laconic Bronson himself. The fact that the Sportster had been owned by Nick, who, presumably, decorated its gas tank with a Masonic symbol, the Eye of Providence, enhances the anthropomorphization of the motorcycle as costar—the Sportster serves as an understudy for Martin Sheen.

Though the pilot episode of the series aired on March 24, 1969, and the film *Easy Rider* wasn't released until July 14 of that year, the television series has been wrongly criticized for being an imitation of the film. There are enough similarities in the plots to see why people could make that mistake. Both feature enigmatic lead characters who set out on a quest to find themselves aboard Harley-Davidson motorcycles, thus both represent twentieth-century interpretations of the mythical American cowboy archetype.

But there are differences, too. The characters in *Easy Rider* find themselves as much through consciousness-expanding drugs, prostitutes, and persecution from and ultimately crucifixion at the hands of rednecks as they do through their motorcycle journey across America. Bronson avoids crucifixion and psychotropic substances, instead finding himself through adventures and helping the people he meets in his travels.

The very first scene of the series proved the most memorable. While escaping from the city and whatever demons are haunting him, Bronson pulls up beside a sleepy commuter in a Chrysler wagon.

"Taking a trip?" the driver asks.
"Yeah," Bronson replies.
"Where to?"
"Oh, I don't know. Wherever I end up, I guess."
"Man, I wish I was you," the driver says.
"Really?"
"Yeah."
"Well," says Bronson, "hang in there."

Then Came Bronson only aired for one season, covering 26 episodes (plus the pilot). Its final episode aired April 1, 1970. The show didn't hang in there long enough to become a staple in syndication, but it managed to attain cult status nonetheless, influencing people as disparate as Bob Seeger and Quentin Tarantino.

THE REHABILITATED CINEMATIC BIKER

By 1985, the image of the biker on film had more or less been rehabilitated. His days of raping and rampaging behind him, the cinematic biker archetype was now a full-fledged sympathetic antihero. No film portrays this sensitive new biker archetype better than *Mask*.

Set in California in the late 1970s, the plot is based on the true story of Roy L. "Rocky" Dennis, a young man who suffered from craniodiaphyseal dysplasia, a rare bone disorder that causes calcium to build up in the skull, disfiguring his facial features and reducing his life expectancy. Because of his horribly disfigured face, the film version of Rocky (played by Eric Stoltz) is ostracized by his peers, but he is accepted unconditionally by his mother, Rusty (played by Cher), as well as by her boyfriend Gar (Sam Elliott) and his band of brothers in the Turks Motorcycle Club.

In a complete reversal of roles from biker flicks of yore, the members of the Turks MC are the compassionate good guys, the extended family that helps Rocky lead a fulfilling (if short) life, and the straights—the normal citizens—are the villains who torment Rocky, who fear him, taunt him, and generally try to make his life a living hell.

With the rough-edged-but-kind-hearted motorcycle club guiding him through life, Rocky beats the odds and thrives in school, making friends and even wooing a girlfriend (Laura Dern), who is, blind.

Roy L. Dennis died in 1978, two months shy of his 17th birthday, providing a heart-rending conclusion to a film that too often strays into the melodramatic. But the impact of the film on the image of motorcyclists was profound. The image of Sam Elliott and his club spreading their healing vibrations aboard their Harleys sent more potential customers into Harley-Davidson showrooms than any previous film.

The timing was perfect—Harley had just introduced a relatively reliable, relatively modern motorcycle. The Evolution-powered motorcycles were the perfect mounts for this new breed of Sam Elliott wannabes. When the film came out in 1985, Harley was still struggling to survive, still existing from day to day on the goodwill of its creditors. After the film came out, Harley sales skyrocketed, and, by the end of the decade, the company had regained dominance in the large-displacement cruiser category for the first time since the Japanese invasion in the 1960s.

SONS OF ANARCHY

In some ways, the on-screen biker archetype had become *too* rehabilitated; by the twenty-first century the cinematic biker had become so Bowdlerized that he'd come to occupy the role of whacky-but-harmless next-door neighbor in a bad sitcom. In 2007, the biker archetype hit rock-bottom in the cringeworthy *Wild Hogs*. This film, which was basically a midnight basketball league for washed-up actors like John Travolta and Tim Allen, was so bad that the writers didn't even bother to create an original plot. Instead, they lifted a page from *The Wild Angels* and had the main characters set out on a quest to retrieve a stolen motorcycle. Unfortunately none of the characters has the good sense to expire on a Nazi flag-draped bed like The Loser.

The bad-boy image of the outlaw biker desperately needed reviving. A year after the release of *Wild Hogs*, *Sons of Anarchy* came along and did just that. *Sons of Anarchy* followed the exploits of a fictional California motorcycle club of the same name.

Covering topics such as vigilantism, government corruption, and racism, *Sons of Anarchy* was as

gritty and violent as *The Sopranos* and *The Wire*. David Labrava and Sonny Barger, actual members of the Hells Angels Motorcycle Club, served as technical advisors, adding to the realistic atmosphere of the series. Even with that, *Sons of Anarchy* has often been criticized for being an unrealistic portrayal of the life Harley-Davidson. Truthfully, it's not a realistic portrayal of that life; as a show about motorcycling, it fell a bit flat. But as a dramatic presentation, it succeeded spectacularly.

Like *West Side Story*, Sons of Anarchy is more of a modern interpretation of a Shakespearean drama than a factual account of life. *West Side Story* emulates the plot of *Romeo and Juliet,* in which Romeo Montague falls in love with Juliet Capulet, initiating an affair that is doomed from the start because the two families are engaged in a longstanding feud. *West Side Story* substitutes the Jets and the Sharks—two warring New York street gangs—for the Montague and Capulet families, but otherwise stays fairly true to the plot of Shakespeare's play.

Sons of Anarchy takes its inspiration from a different Shakespearean play: *Hamlet*. The motorcycle-mounted twenty-first-century Hamlet

is Jackson "Jax" Teller, played by Charlie Hunnam. The Jax character marks a return to the Brando-style brooding rebel biker; unlike Brando's Johnny, who was rebelling against "what do you got?", Jax's melancholia has a very specific source—the death of his father, the founding president of the Sons of Anarchy MC. This, incidentally, is the same source of Hamlet's depression, only Hamlet's father was the king of Denmark and not the president of a gun-running motorcycle club.

The similarities don't end there. Though Jax's father doesn't make a ghostly appearance, as does Hamlet's father, he does play the role of *deus ex machina* in the form of a book, a manifesto of sorts that the deceased father wrote to explain himself to his then-newborn son.

Like *Hamlet*'s mother Gertrude, Jax's mother Gemma (played by Katey Sagal) has married her late husband's brother, Clay Morrow (Ron Perlman). That Clay is a club brother rather than a brother by blood is incidental in the world of motorcycle clubs. It turns out that, as in *Hamlet*, Jax's mother and stepfather murdered Jax's father. And, also as in *Hamlet* (and pretty much every other Shakespearean drama), everyone (with the possi-

ble exception of Rosencrantz and Guildenstern) dies at the end, but not before taking viewers on one hell of a ride.

Sons of Anarchy premiered on September 3, 2008, and ran until December 9, 2014, becoming the highest-rated television series in the history of cable television along the way. The extremely well-developed characters, violent criminals though they were, captured viewers' affection.

The motorcycle action itself seemed a bit contrived and unrealistic to any experienced motorcyclist, and the criminal aspect of the club was highly exaggerated for dramatic effect, but the writing, dialog, acting, and action were of the highest quality. Throughout the series, characters were never presented in Hellenistic duality; there were no good guys or bad guys—though some characters were more good than others and some characters more bad, all were fleshed out and well rounded. Viewers felt at least some pity for characters who came to well-deserved bad ends and were never quite comfortable when other characters didn't pay for their sins. They cheered when the club murdered a corrupt federal agent and when Jax beat a sadistic pris-

on guard to death in the man's own kitchen (after murdering the man's wife in cold blood), because the plot was so well developed that viewers clearly understood the characters' motivation.

The one thing the characters in *Sons of Anarchy* were not was rehabilitated (though Jax often toyed with the idea of taking his wife and family far away from the criminal life). The Sons of Anarchy were not some cuddly, teddy-bear bikers on a toy run, though they could fool onlookers into believing they were.

And they weren't really motorcyclists. Rather, they were members of a criminal enterprise that also happened to be a motorcycle club. But it didn't matter; except for hardcore motorcyclists who bristled at some of the absurd crash scenes and members of real motorcycle clubs who took umbrage at the portrayal of a motorcycle club as a criminal enterprise, most people loved the series. The motorcycle aspect may have been secondary to the on-screen action, but the characters and plot were so compelling that they motivated a new generation to enter the life Harley-Davidson.

EPILOGUE: FREEDOM

Ultimately the life Harley-Davidson is about one thing: freedom. It might seem a bit clichéd, but it's also true. It was just as true for Bill Harley and the Davidson boys in 1903 as it is for Norman Reedus today. Nothing equals the sense of freedom you find while riding a motorcycle. When you shift your bike into gear and head out on the open road, you leave everything else behind. On a motorcycle, the worries of everyday life fall away and you exist only in that moment; the universe is reduced to the razor's edge between you and your bike and the world rushing toward you. Riding a motorcycle is such an intense activity that there's no room for anything else to creep in. You're overwhelmed by the sights, sounds, and smells coming at you. Once you've let the experience of riding a bike drive all the useless thoughts from your head, you really start to understand the concept of freedom. You enter a magical world where time has little meaning; it's just you, your bike, and the road.

Welcome to
the life Harley-Davidson.

PAGE 134-135

Mick Jagger looks on as Hells Angel Alan Passaro stabs Meredith Hunter in front of the stage during the Altamont Speedway Free Festival on December 6, 1969. Hunter had stormed the stage waving a .22-caliber revolver. Passaro was acquitted of murder and possibly saved Jagger's (or another band member's) life.

PAGE 130-131

Ralph Hubert "Sonny" Barger came to national prominence after the publication of Hunter S. Thompson's book *Hells Angels: The Strange and Terrible Saga of the Outlaw Motorcycle Gangs*. This author worked with both men. When I asked Hunter about Sonny, Hunter said, "Sonny and I have made our peace." When I asked Sonny about Hunter, Sonny said, "Did he tell you what he did when the cops raided our party?" I said *no*. "He took a twelve-pack of beer and locked himself in the trunk of his car."

PAGE 132-133

Though the presence of the Hells Angels at Altamont possibly saved someone from dying at the hands of Meredith Hunter, overall they contributed to making a very bad scene even worse. Not only did the Angels thump the audience, at one point they beat up Jefferson Airplane singer Marty Balin on stage. The Angels didn't just preserve disorder; they created it.

PAGE 152-153

In 1987 Deborah Beall, a thirty-year-old mother of two, threatened to sue the Hells Angels if the club didn't reverse its "males only" policy and allow women to become members.

PAGE 170-171

The Chingalings, a Puerto Rican motorcycle club, in front of their South Bronx clubhouse on January 15, 1975.

PAGE 164-165

A member of the Outlaws MC crosses the Ohio River aboard his Panhead bobber.

PAGE 168-169

Black Panthers cofounder Bobby Seale (second from left) traveling to Attica State Correctional Facility on September 11, 1971, to take part in a citizens panel intermediating between the prisoners and state officials.

PAGE 160-161

The Outlaws clubhouse in Dayton, Ohio, 1965.

PAGE 162-163

A gathering of Outlaws, Elkhorn, Wisconsin, 1965.

PAGE 158-159

Girlfriends of Hells Angels members relax aboard their boyfriends' Harleys during a ride from San Bernardino to Bakersfield. This photo was taken in 1965, the year Thompson was writing *Hells Angels: The Strange and Terrible Saga of the Outlaw Motorcycle Gangs*.

Terrible Saga of the Outlaw Motorcycle Gangs, which chronicled his experiences with the club.

PAGE 180-181

This is the photo that exposed America to the motorcycle menace. Photographer Barney Peterson captured this image of Eddie Davenport, a member of a club called the Tulare Riders, enjoying a refreshing beverage (or two) aboard his Flathead at Hollister the night of the July 4, 1947 disturbance.

PAGE 150-151

Members of the Outlaw MC gather outside Kitty's Saloon, the club's clubhouse, on November 26, 1967. Florida Governor Claude Kirk had Kitty's shut down following a case in which five members of the club had beaten nineteen-year-old Christine Deese and nailed her to a tree in Juniper, Florida, because Deese allegedly owed $10 to club member Norman "Spider" Risinger.

PAGE 196-197

Brigitte Bardot posed aboard a Harley-Davidson during a performance of singer-provocateur Serge Gainsbourg's song, "Harley David Son-of-a-Bitch."

PAGE 62-63

A lifelong Harley-Davidson rider, musician Rockie Lynne has appeared nationally on *Good Morning America*, *Fox and Friends*, *ABC News*, and has appeared many times on the stage of the Grand Ole Opry. Rockie is a member of Rolling Thunder, a veteran's advocacy group founded by the Vietnam Veterans MC, and is the headline entertainer every year at the annual Rolling Thunder demonstration in Washington, D.C., on Memorial Day weekend.

PAGE 206-207

Hunter S. Thompson earned a reputation as a brilliant political commentator but he first gained fame as the author of *Hells Angels: The Strange and*

PAGE 24-25

The first official military purchase of Harley-Davidsons came in 1916, when General John "Blackjack" Pershing ordered 12 motorcycles to aid in his pursuit of Pancho Villa along the Mexican border. These four soldiers were among the lucky recipients of those machines.

PAGE 92-93

Between 1925 and the 1960 trade embargo, Harley exported more than 100 motorcycles to Cuba, many of which remain in operation today. Because the importation of spare parts is illegal, resourceful Cuban mechanics have kept the motorcycles running by adapting parts from Soviet automobiles to replace the original Harley-Davidson components.

PAGE 10-11

Though she stood just four-feet-eleven and weighed only 88 pounds, Sally Halterman (shown here aboard a 1929-31 Model W) wasn't intimidated by the phallocentric culture surrounding Harley-Davidson. In 1913, the 27-year-old became the first female to earn a license to operate a motorcycle in the District of Columbia.

PAGE 96-97

Honda's CB750 eclipsed the Sportster as a performance machine in 1969, but in 1966 the XCLCH was still one of the fastest motorcycles available.

PAGE 80-81

Joe D. Hunter and Clara Lee Bell (Hunter), 1937. Photo taken near Aledo, Texas.

PAGE 120-121

Ann-Margret (shown here riding a Triumph chopper in the Nevada desert on New Year's Day, 1969) starred opposite Joe Nameth in the biker flick *CC and Company*. Critics savaged the film, though none in quite so sleazy a fashion as Gene Siskel, who wrote, "Ann-Margret has a brief nude scene in which she proves that in addition to having a foul mouth she is fat." Proving empirically that Gene Siskel really was an asshole—it wasn't our imaginations.

PAGE 146-147

A group of Hells Angels and their girlfriends hang out in front of the Blackboard Café in Bakersfield, 1965.

PAGE 144-145

New buyers flocked to the new and reliable Evolution-powered Harleys by the tens of thousands, but old-school Harley riders resented these newbies and their expensive motorcycles, a sentiment expressed on t-shirts as, "Hear no Evo, Speak no Evo, Ride no Evo!"

PAGE 112-113

Indian MP Ranjeet Ranjan arrives at Parliament House on International Women's Day, March 8, 2016, aboard her Harley-Davidson. Ranjan made international headlines on August 21, 2017, when her convoy was involved in an incident in which three people were crushed to death.

PAGE 142-143

The State Police arrived at Hollister brandishing automatic weapons—apparently expecting World War III—but the actual scene they encountered was tamer than expected.

INDEX

I'D LIKE TO THANK THE MOTORBOOKS TEAM, PUBLISHER ZACK MILLER AND PROJECT MANAGERS, JORDAN WIKLUND, ALYSSA BLUHM, AND NYLE VIALET, FOR ALL THEIR WORK ON THIS PROJECT, AS WELL AS MINNEAPOLIS GROUP PUBLISHER ERIK GILG FOR CONCEIVING OF AND MAKING THIS SERIES OF BOOKS HAPPEN. I'D ESPECIALLY LIKE TO THANK CREATIVE DIRECTOR LAURA DREW AND DESIGNER BETH MIDDLEWORTH WHO WORKED RELENTLESSLY TO MAKE THIS THE COOLEST-LOOKING BOOK I'VE EVER SEEN.